5 Steps to School Success:
Plus, Tips for Improving Communication with Teachers

By Julie C. Gilbert

Aletheia Pyralis Publishers

For information about special discounts available for bulk purchases, sales promotions, fund-raising and educational needs, please email: juliecgilbert5steps@gmail.com.

http://www.juliecgilbert.com/
https://sites.google.com/view/juliecgilbert-writer/

Love Science Fiction or Mystery?

Choose your adventure!

Visit: http://www.juliecgilbert.com/

For details on getting free books

Dedication:

To each class that's asked me "are we your favorite?"

Answer 1: I don't do favorites.
Answer 2: Yes, you are all my favorite.
Answer 3: Every class is my favorite in their own special way.

Special Thanks:
Tim Sparvero for the excellent illustrations.
http://www.infinityroads.com/commission-me/

Table of Contents:

Introduction:

Dear High School or College Student (and his/her parent or guardian),

Who is this book for and how should you use it?

The book is mainly aimed at students entering high school, but anybody still in high school (or the equivalent) or starting college should be able to get something useful out of it.

The first chapters will expand on the basic steps I think you'll need to take to be a successful student. Beyond that, I'll dive more specifically into other related topics that tie back into the steps. There is a method to my madness in the way it's organized, but everything should be pretty modular. So, if you need to focus on a specific area, go for it.

To that end, it might be best to get whichever version you can best take notes on, be that ebook or paperback. Audio's great if you're an auditory learner, but if that's not you, don't bother.

Life's going to pull you in different directions. Best be prepared for it.

High School

Part Time Job

Parents

Life

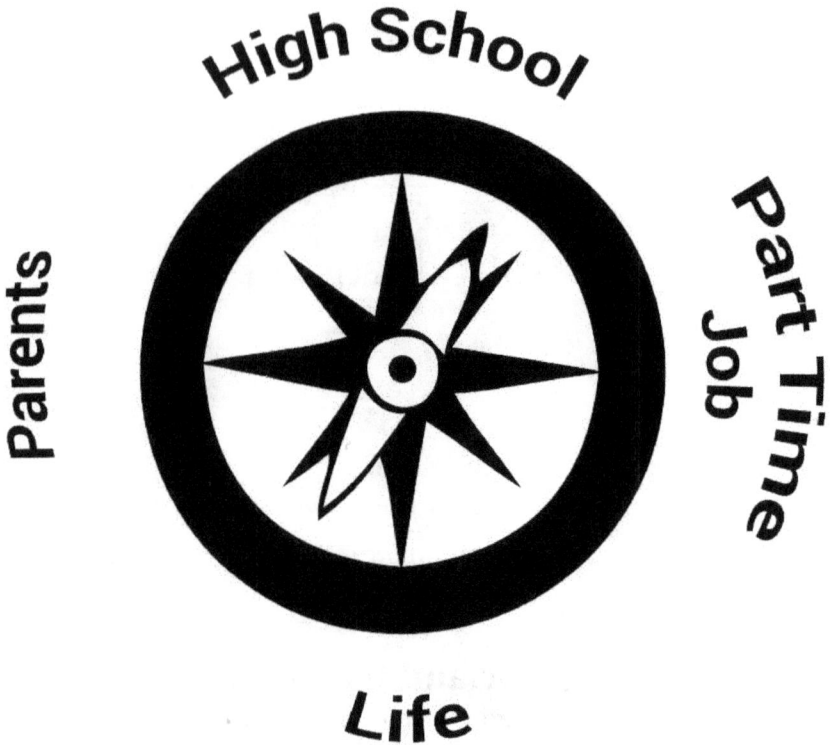

What this book is not?

It's not a guarantee you'll earn straight A's in class. If properly applied, you should be able to maximize your academic performance, but hopefully, I can convince you there's so much more to high school than grades. Before you throw the book, consider it might be your iPhone or a very expensive kindle.

It's not simply going to be a shopping list of common-sense platitudes. It might start that way, but I also intend to give you insider information on how your teachers think. First bit of wisdom up in those platitude-like statements, strive to do your best and improve, but don't hold yourself to an impossible standard.

The book will not have all the answers. Wish that were possible, but school can take so many different forms. While much can be applicable to any educational institution or situation, schools vary in size and resources. Individual student situations have endless variations.

Who am I and why should you care what I have to say?

I'm a high school Chemistry teacher and a multi-genre writer. I've worked in both the public and private sectors as well as done my share of tutoring and summer school programs. You don't really need to know how many years I've been doing this job, but suffice to say, I have learned a lot thus far yet still have far to go. I've worked with every level of high schooler as well as fifth graders. (That was a strange time in my life.)

Why is this book important?

I see about a dozen books on this topic (doing well in school), but so far, very few, if any, of them are written by teachers. While it's awesome that there are multiple perspectives on the topic, I think it'll be helpful for you to get a teacher's perspective.

School dominates the first major chunk of your life. It's here that you'll develop the habits and attitudes that will shape not only the kind of worker but also the kind of person you'll be later in life. At the risk of sounding sappy, I'd like to help you become a well-rounded, critical thinker who has the confidence and knowhow to make the most of high school.

What is school and why do I have to be here?

Short Answer:
Because the powers that be said so.

Longer Answer:
Ideally, school should be a place for people to grow and learn. It should be a safe environment to discover oneself.

In reality, it can be a social jungle where there are constant power struggles and feelings get hurt.

5 Steps to School Success:

Step #1: Gain Good Perspective
Step #2: Manage Your Time Well
Step #3: Persist and Persevere
Step #4: Build a Solid Class Reputation
Step #5: Communicate Effectively with Everybody, Especially Your Teachers

5 Steps to School Success: (The annotated version ...)

Step #1: Gain Good Perspective

In most countries, you must go to school. It's your job, and there are varying consequences for your parents if you choose not to go. But you shouldn't see it as an obligation. See it as an opportunity. You are privileged to receive an education. In many cases, that education even comes without costs. Sometimes, it even comes with free or reduced lunches, depending on your family's economic situation. That's a double-edge sword of contention, but I'm going to skip that debate for now. Point is this: school will likely be your first step into the wider world. Make the most of it.

Step #2: Manage Your Time Well

Time is a strange thing. As you get older, it will seem to speed up. American culture pushes hard for being involved in everything. The concept's not going to be a hard sell, so most of the chapter will revolve around the ways to find what works for you so you can make the most of the limited time you have. In other words, I'm going to give you suggestions on how you can study smarter, not harder.

Step #3: Persist and Persevere

A quick Google search would give you formal definitions for persistence and perseverance. To me, the former has to do with pushing forward to accomplish what you need to do, and the latter has more to do with recovering from a setback. Both skills will aid you on your quest to not only survive but to thrive at school. You'll need to be able to identify when you're stressed and learn how to cope with it in order to conquer it. Coping and conquering with stress or setbacks can take many forms, but some are healthier and more productive than others.

Step #4: Build a Solid Class Reputation
There's an ancient concept that you reap what you sow. You might be tempted to think, *I'm a kid. Nobody cares how I act.* But the attitudes you develop now will shape the actions you take and those can come back to haunt you or set you up for success. First, I aim to show you the multitude of little things that can add or detract from your class reputation. After that, I will describe some of the benefits of having a solid class reputation.

Step #5: Communicate Effectively with Everybody, Especially Your Teachers
I'm an introvert, so dealing with people in person can be draining. As such, email and other written forms of communication are preferable to phone calls or face-to-face meetings. That said, it's best you become proficient at communicating your thoughts, questions, and ideas as effectively as possible in multiple mediums.

Bonus Information:

Bonus 1: Reading your teacher
Bonus 2: Picking the right battles
Bonus 3: How to ask for things
Bonus 4: Useful skills
Bonus 5: Seeking help and navigating resources
Bonus 6: Writing great emails
Bonus 7: Wise words from parents, teachers, and students

Conclusion:

Being a student can be difficult. Let's face it, life can be difficult. You can't control all the crazy around you, but you can control your actions and reactions. My main goal in writing this book is to provide tips, tricks, and hints that will make your life easier, letting you have a more enjoyable high school (or college) experience.

Part 1:
The 5 Steps

Chapter 1:
Gain Good Perspective

Introduction:

At the risk of being a teacher cliché, I'm going to open with a motivational speech. Since time's a precious commodity, I will strive to say only what's necessary so as not to waste any of your time. This chapter will first attempt to convince you of the necessity of the right mindset concerning school. Next, the focus will shift to the decisions you need to consciously make to strike a nice balance between academics and your social, emotional, and physical well-being. It's more of an overview. Details and suggested how-to's will come in subsequent chapters.

Change "Got to" to "Get to" – Power of Positivity and All that Rot

Some students love school. Others do not. Some may even hate school. Wherever you fall on the love-hate school spectrum, odds are good you're required to be there. You might as well make the most of the situation. The first step involves changing your mindset. Stop viewing school as the obligation it is and start seeing it as a nearly endless stream of opportunities to prove yourself, interact with people, and learn stuff. I can almost guarantee you the vast majority of lessons you learn from high school won't be related to the actual subject matter you're studying in class.

The Importance of Good Balance:

Life's like a video game. I might regret making that analogy later but hear me out. Many games force you to balance energy and activity. Usually, there are resources you need to gain in order to build or buy something that improves your world or moves you closer to your quest goals. Other, more action-based games have you collect things that give you money or energy or something to do magic with. You slay weak enemies to gain the resources to obtain better weapons to face stronger foes. Point is, unless you've got a cheat code, you need to work up to facing the end bosses. You also need to build a balanced character.

Let's run with the video game analogy for a while. Your school life contains four aspects or areas to balance: academics, social, emotional, and physical. If you throw every scrap of energy and effort into one area, likely you're doing so to the detriment of another area. Unlike a video game, when it comes to your life, you get one shot at this.

You probably have some control over which extracurricular activities you get involved in, but I'm sure your parents had some significant input as well. Each type of activity and club has benefits for one or more of the school aspects. Sports offer physical and social benefits. Social clubs involve many opportunities to interact with those who have similar interests. Academic clubs let you go beyond the classroom, which usually makes the learning more fun. Depending on your needs, any one of these types of clubs and activities can have emotional benefits.

As you get older, you'll begin to have more control over which courses you take. Once you have that control, it's important that you select a load that's challenging but not overwhelming. Where those lines lie will largely depend on you. By the time you reach high school, you should be able to take a decent stab at predicting how much you can reasonably handle and still function.

Overview of the School Arenas:
Arena 1: Academics
Level of control: high

There's probably a stuffy definition somewhere, but I'm going to use this term to refer to anything related to the paper-pushing, test-taking, project-performing side of school. Every few years the Ivy Tower know-it-alls hand down a "new" way that school absolutely *MUST* be done! They cycle back and forth between fundamentals and going-with-the-flow sorts of theories. Regardless of the flavor of the year, there's always some kind of work to be done in school.

As I said, being a student is your current job. You just happen to be paid by grades based on the quality of the work. Some people absolutely love this aspect of school. I can see it being the most straightforward. If the instructions are clear, there's usually little chance for something academic to turn around and bite you, paper cuts aside. Once you learn the spoken and unspoken rules, this can be the easiest aspect to master.

Arena 2: Social Interactions
Level of control: high

The social scene has the potential to be one of the more unpredictable minefields that exist in schools. But there's good news. You can usually control who you hang out with. Surround yourself with people who have similar interests, challenge you to be better, and will support you through thick and thin. Learn to be comfortable with your own company, but don't avoid other people.

Unless the world drastically changes, there will always be people with bullying mentalities and tendencies. They seek to dominate others to prove they're better than everybody else. Ignore such people as best you can. Conversely, if you're up for a challenge, you can try to befriend them and change them by the force of your charismatic personality. Keep in mind that bullies usually developed that part of themselves as a defense mechanism against some sort of pain. Certainly, don't become one yourself.

Arena 3: Emotional Health
Level of control: medium
I've ranked the amount of control you have over your emotional health as medium because life can and will occasionally throw curveballs. These events can be good or bad. Both have the potential to tax your emotional reserves. Family members can get sick. Accidents can claim loved ones. Families break apart. New siblings come into the world. Broken families get combined and melded together into new families.

Be aware of your stress levels and find beneficial ways to ease them. This might take some work. There are almost as many ways to de-stress as stressors that can crop up in your life. Any list I can compile will only begin to scratch the surface of possibilities. You might have to do some trial and error to find what works for you. I'll expand on these ideas in the chapter focused on persistence and perseverance.

You can't control everything. Don't try to, and don't despair at the lack of control. Picture your emotional health like a river you're kayaking down. The paddle gives you some control, but your job is to steer with the river currents, not fight them. Fighting the currents will only exhaust you. Redirecting and adjusting are your best bets for dealing with the unpredictable twists and turns the river throws your way. Same's true in life.

Arena 4: Physical Health
Level of control: medium
Some people live for physical activity. Exercise excites and energizes them. Not me. I have to be purposeful about taking walks, and I really only manage it regularly during the summer months. Other than that, I have a job that keeps me on my feet a lot. I'd rate my personal dedication to maintaining physical health as medium to low. Most students should get some physical activity from running around from class to class, attending physical education class, and participating in a sport. Some people walk to school. Others have to be purposeful about exercising.

Eating right falls into this category too. Time can be an enemy to eating right. Sometimes, it's finance. Sometimes, it's choice. If you have control over the situation, wonderful. If you don't, do the best with what you're given.

Balancing the Arenas of Life

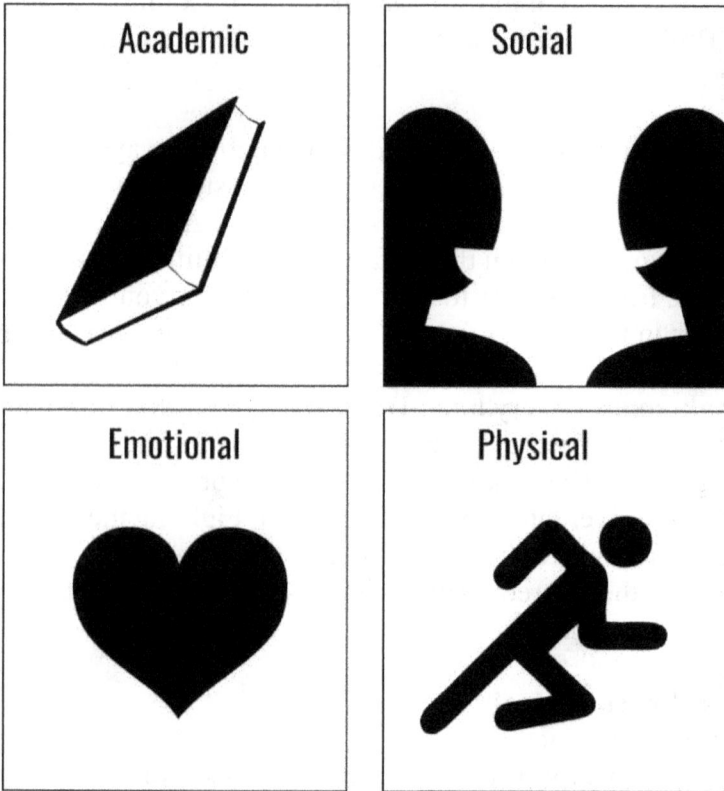

Academic	Social

Emotional	Physical

Conclusion:

School can be a place to make lifelong friends, learn about how the world works, and interact with others in a relatively safe environment. Letting any one aspect of school life dominate can cause the others to suffer.

Chapter 2:
Time Well Spent

Introduction:

Time matters. Unless you're purposeful about spending time well, it will pass in a blink with little to nothing to show for it. Most people will need to spend some time on their academics in order to do well. There are rare people who can breeze through a class if they pay half attention, but they will eventually meet their match somewhere. Cultivating great study habits now will serve you well throughout your career as a student.

Find Out How You Learn Best:

You don't need to hear buzzwords like kinesthetic learning to know if you gravitate to doing stuff as a means of absorbing material. Auditory learners take in information as they hear it. Visual learners comprehend best when seeing something. Smell and taste may also be associated with information. That might sound weird, but it can happen. Once, when I was a kid, I read a book about John Newton while eating a large bag of Skittles. To this day, that particular candy kind of reminds me of that book. (That was back when lime flavored ones were included in regular Skittles packs.)

Try out some of the study tools and tricks below. Mix them up.

Although you might have a primary or preferred way of learning, you'll be able to absorb information from the other methods, albeit to a lesser extent. Find a combination that works for you.

Common Study Tools and Tricks:

Notes: Most American high schools still favor visual and auditory learners. There's a big push to make things more accessible for those who learn different ways, but traditional notetaking is still a valued skill. Some students are naturally more gifted in this area. I was not one of them. My handwriting's terrible unless I'm going super slow. I color coded and rewrote my notes after each day. These days, you might be able to take faster notes by typing. Keep in mind that the physical act of forming the words with a pen put to paper could be the thing helping you learn, so don't just skip to the easier method because you think it'll be a shortcut.

Notecards/Flashcards: Some teachers will make you create physical notecards to learn vast quantities of information. Others will tell you to make virtual flashcards online. Still others won't give you instructions one way or another. You may have to choose to do this on your own. This tactic works best on things like vocabulary lists or chapter definitions for science class.

Uncommon Study Tools and Tricks:

Audio Notes: Technology has moved to a point where taking audio notes is easier than ever. There are free apps for most phones that will allow you to record a certain number of minutes of information. If you need more storage space, you could do the same or better with a computer and a webcam. Read through your notes and play it back later, or with permission from your teacher, record the lecture portions of the class.

Video Notes: This is another method that wasn't available to me as a high school student. We had video cameras, of course, but they were bulky, hand-held things not easily applied to a school setting. You likely don't have that issue, unless of course, budget concerns limit your resources.

Record yourself reading through your notes and illustrating certain points. Check with your teacher. See if he or she has any video resources already created for you. In addition, you can search YouTube for videos already made for the topic you're trying to learn.

Caution: There's very little quality control on some of these videos. You might be given incorrect information. Learn to evaluate the effectiveness of the video.

The easiest way to find an educational video is to try a few search terms in YouTube.

How to determine if a YouTube video is trustworthy:
- Look at the number of views and the release date. Compare the number of views to those of similar videos. It's not necessarily about what has the most views but that can be a good indicator the video is legitimate and helpful. I mean there are probably videos of cats yawning that have a few million views, but aside from maybe de-stressing you, that's not going to help with your study session. A low number of views doesn't necessarily translate to trash though.

- Check the release date. Sometimes, things take time to gather a following. The importance of the date will vary based on the topic you're researching. For example, a chemistry video might be eight years old but still valid. Conversely, a political news video could be a few months old and horribly outdated.
- You may also want to check out the comments. If there are a few thousand comments, you certainly don't have to read them all but skim a few. If they're mostly of the thank-you-for-saving-my-skin type, then you should be good to go concerning the trustworthiness of the video.
- You could always ask your teacher to review the video. Not everybody responds to email communication and some may resent being given extra work. If you can't get a teacher to review the video for you, ask a friend or a sibling who took the course already or is currently doing well in the class.
- See if past videos by the same producer are helpful. This won't work if it's week one, but if you're a few months into the school year, give it a go. Find a topic you've already got a decent grasp on and watch a few videos by various creators. If you can find a reliable content creator, you should be fine to trust the information they're giving you about a new topic.

Tactile Tricks: I used to do a lot of my studying with a plastic lightsaber in hand. I also did a fair amount of pacing. It's hard to say how much the tactic helped me study, but at the very least, the movement helped me maintain my focus. Sometimes, I would flip the lightsaber or toss it back and forth between my hands. Other times, I would just swing it around for a few seconds. The object you hold doesn't have to be a lightsaber. I liked it because it had some heft to it, was durable, and had a few configurations. Pens, lip balm, stress balls, hair ties, and other small objects can work too.

If you can do it safely, you might consider taking a walk while studying. Try building models out of simple household items. Make up signals or hand gestures that remind you of the topic. Create a memory game out of flashcards. Grab some Legos or some other building toy and use the various colors or shapes to represent something you're studying. Get a mini-basketball set and allow yourself one shot for every question you get right as you study.

Association with Something You Enjoy: Finding out if this method works for you could be fun. Find some music you love or a certain kind of candy and consume it while studying for something. The brain works in mysterious ways. I recommend picking one or the other, not both. The reason goes back to the basics of running an experiment. You only want to mess with one independent variable at a time. Otherwise, you won't know whether it's the music or the candy that's helping you learn. The combination of music and candy might be the magic solution but make that a separate trial in your experiment.
Caution: There's a chance you might ruin that music or candy for yourself. I remember hearing a certain song while studying for a thermochemistry test in college. To this day, that song reminds me of the class. It hasn't completely ruined the song, but I don't go out of my way to hear the song either. Let's just say thermochem wasn't my favorite college class.

Rewards: Consider something you love to do. Set up a small reward system for yourself. The ideas to come are not comprehensive. They're only meant to pique your interest in the idea and prompt your own creativity.

The mini-basketball game mentioned previously falls into this category. Buy a candy bar and take a bite when you reach certain milestones in your studying. Pay yourself an allowance for reaching certain milestones then buy something you like or treat yourself to a dinner out or a movie. Put off playing a video game until you put in a certain amount of study time. Take a ten-minute nap at the end of every hour's worth of studying. If you try this, use an alarm. The method won't work for everybody because not everybody can do power naps. Bake a batch of cookies and reward yourself when you get to a certain point.

Keep Distractions to a Minimum:
You need to take breaks, but you also must keep those breaks from destroying the flow of information. The internet, video games, the wrong kind of music, phones, and people can be distractions. I'm not

necessarily suggesting you study in silence. The right music can aid memorization and help you study better.

The Internet: Your assignment may require you to browse the internet. If you're doing schoolwork on a computer, make a concerted effort to stay off social media sites. It's very easy to get lost browsing something like Facebook or Instagram.

Video Games: Confession time. I play a lot of games on my iPhone both in school and out of school. I'd probably be appalled if I added up the few minutes here and there and found the actual time I spent/ wasted playing a stupid phone game. Console games are worse in terms of the time they take. They're also awesome. You need things in life that you enjoy. The caution I'll leave you with is this: budget for video game time instead of letting it seep into work time.

Music: I typically cannot concentrate enough to study if there are lyrics playing. Some people can. I prefer movie soundtracks that don't have lyrics when I study. I'm sure there's an app out there waiting to let you create a study playlist. You might have to pay for it if you want to avoid ads, but the fee might be worth your sanity. If you can't afford it, don't sweat it. Create a playlist on YouTube. Their commercials are a tad easier to ignore. Find music you can work with. It's supposed to enhance your learning, not detract from it.

Phones: It's hard not to have your phone near you. Guess this one comes down to willpower. If you can have your phone near you and still concentrate, keep it there. If you can't, put it on silent and put it away. There are many reasons to ignore this advice, but at the very least, turn it upside down and turn off flashing and pinging notifications from every social media network that exists. Staying connected to friends is great but spending your study time texting isn't likely to help your grades unless you can confine your conversation to the work at hand.

People: I often tell my students that people make life worth living. Study groups work for some people, but circumstances and time constraints make them tough to arrange while in high school. Depending on the dynamics of your household, you may be able to carve out a place to study in peace or you might be stuck in the middle of controlled chaos. If you can arrange to be at a quiet place like a library, that might help. Noise cancelling headphones might be the only way to disappear into a quiet headspace. In that case, I recommend instrumental music.

Control Your Study Environment: I was lucky enough to have quiet study areas readily available at home or my apartment. If you require the opposite, seek out a place with people, like a coffee shop. Headphones and music may help you control your environment, but even things like where you keep your phone will help with this endeavor. The environment in this section refers to the area immediately around you. Textbooks and study materials may need to be a part of the environment, but for each subject and study session, try to only have what's necessary. If you don't use the textbook, leave it out, unless you want it there for ambiance. You may want a drink or a small snack but try to keep it simple. You don't want something that's going to leave a mark on every paper you touch.

Conclusion:

Combine different study tools, tips, and tricks. Everybody learns differently. Also, certain topics or subjects may be more conducive to some methods over others. There is not a guaranteed fix-all method that works for everyone. I've always gravitated to methods that help with brute force memorization. That's not exactly the best method to learn, but it carried me through most of my high school career. Honestly, the best way to learn something is to teach it, but that's a bit difficult to do while learning something the first time.

Rewriting notes and reviewing them while pacing and carrying a lightsaber worked for me. Video and audio notes were harder to do back in my schooling days. You'll have to experiment a bit to see what's most comfortable for you. Adapt to the moment. If one method frustrates you, try another. If you physically or financially can't afford a certain method, skip it. Make up your own method.

Chapter 3:
Persist and Persevere

Introduction:

Setbacks will happen. Life will do everything in its power to throw you off balance. Expect it. Anticipate it. I won't say relish it, though some people enjoy the excitement of uncertainty. At the very least, learn from each experience. Keeping your stress levels under control will help you handle setbacks when they come. I'm going to define perseverance as the ability to endure unpleasantness with grace such that you can continue to perform your duties to a high degree. In short, it's pushing through the bad stuff. Persistence will help you persevere and having low stress will allow you the emotional capacity to persist when necessary.

What's Stress Got to Do with It?

Have you ever played a video game where you must sneak around without being noticed? There's usually a bar somewhere on the screen that will measure how much attention you're gaining. Sometimes, you need to keep still to let the bar decrease to a safe level. If that bar gets too high, you get busted. Picture your stress levels like this. It's to your advantage to keep stress as low as possible so that when something distinctly stressful happens, you can handle the spike in level.

How do you keep your stress levels low?

This isn't a weight loss plan. I can't assign numbers to each type of de-stressor. Though that would be kind of fun, the truth remains that the values I would assign might differ for you based on personal preference. Best I can do is break them down into categories and let you choose your favorites. There's always a tradeoff between the destressor and the time investment. Find something that relaxes you without adding to the burdens you already bear.

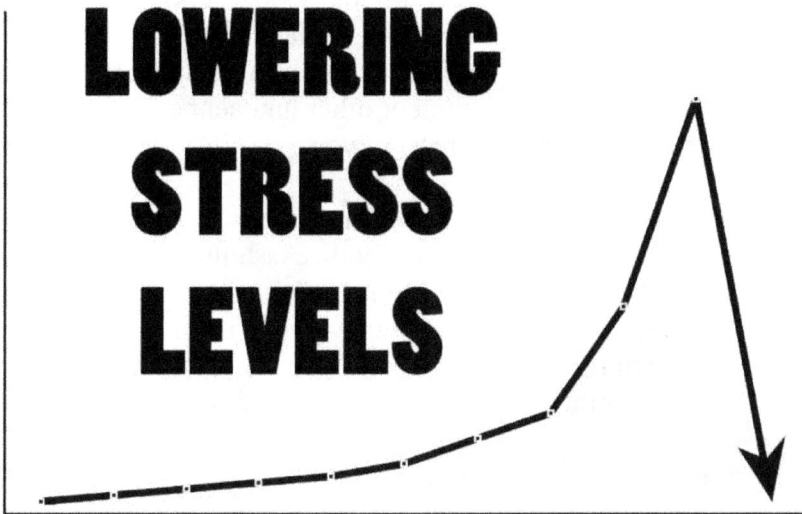

LOWERING STRESS LEVELS

Ways to Unwind:

Exercise: Whether we're talking organized sports or personal initiative, exercising takes a lot of time. If you like moving, this would be an appealing way to forget your troubles. I could expound on the chemical response your body has to physical activity, but it's not my area of expertise, so the information would be no deeper than the nearest Google page. What I can say is that this one isn't for everybody. Exercise tends to be more of a chore for me. Sure, it feels great when it's over, but I don't enjoy the process of getting disgustingly sweaty.

Music: Time varies, but even though each song isn't terribly long, it's easy to get lost in a playlist. There's a song for everything, but not every song is conducive to relaxing or dealing with stress. Music can evoke emotions, so be careful about what you choose when trying to unwind. Filling your head with something that will get you pumped up and ready to conquer the world may or may not be the right choice for you. Same for slow and sad. Maybe mellow tunes can ground you. Classic rock might work too.

Find something that makes you feel good without being a bad influence. Would you be embarrassed to play the song in front of your whole family from your grandmother down to a little baby cousin? If it's not suitable for small children or other innocent ears, it's probably not great for relaxing and destressing you.

Movies and TV Shows: Unless you have iron willpower, this one can be time-consuming, expensive, or both. Assuming you can legally access movies, this may be a way to forget your troubles by becoming immersed in a fictional character's woes. Television shows tend to be shorter, either a half-hour, forty-two minutes, or an hour. With Netflix and Amazon and other studios that have streaming services running their own programs, that timing might differ, but TV shows are usually more manageable than movies.

Once again, your tastes might differ, but I think certain genres are better suited to relaxing. Mindless action and light comedy fit the bill better than dark, twisty psychological thrillers or horror shows. When trying to temporarily leave this world for a fictional one, it's best if you don't have to invest too much brainpower in figuring things out.

Books and Audiobooks: A cheaper way to experience stories involves books and audiobooks. Both have their place. Audiobooks are easier because somebody's reading to you. This frees you to do something else like build Legos, take a walk, get some chores done, or work on a puzzle. They tend to be more expensive since production costs for that medium are higher. However, most libraries have some audiobooks on CD or available as an online resource with your library subscription. The choices might be limited, but it's a great place to start.

With libraries and community book sales, physical books are cheap. Choices may be limited depending on the budget of your local library. Also, if you have a kindle and keep to the right Facebook groups, you can probably pick up a lot of free books. Same is true for audiobooks. Audible gives authors and narrators codes to promote their books and generate reviews. If you're willing to review stories, you can have an endless supply of them.

The same general principles apply to books and audiobooks as with movies. Choose something lighter on the scale. There's a time for dark and twisty tales, but lighthearted and amusing works better for forgetting the problems that plague you.

Friends: Be cautious with this one. Friends can often cause as much stress as they're capable of relieving. I can't tell you how to make friends, but I will encourage you to keep track of your own mental and emotional health when it comes to dealing with friends. This does not mean you abandon people just because they have heavy stuff going on in their lives, but if you come across someone whose negativity permeates the atmosphere, you might want to keep your distance. You want to surround yourself with a small group of core people who will be there for you when you need a distraction, advice, or a sympathetic ear. Commiserating with somebody who understands exactly what you're dealing with can go a long way in keeping you sane.

Cleaning: Don't knock it until you've tried it. Cleaning and organizing can be excellent ways to handle stress. It's productive, necessary, and potentially cathartic (emotionally releasing). It allows you to bring order to a kind of chaos you have full control over. A large part of the power behind most stressors is a lack of control over a situation. Uncertainty. Cleaning narrows the focus of the world temporarily by pitting you and your cleaning supplies against dirt and dust, something you can see and feel.

Craft, Cook, or Create: Paints, pencils, puzzles, and pans are excellent tools for relaxing. Physical puzzles are nice because, like cleaning, they illustrate order coming out of chaos. For those with the skill, painting and drawing can be immensely relaxing. Cooking or baking can also fulfill the need to create something from nothing. The key here is to spend time doing something you enjoy that has a tangible result you can be proud of.

Enjoying Nature: There may be some crossover here between enjoying nature and exercising. Cost for this one tends to be low, but that depends heavily on accessibility. Even if you live in a city, there's usually a nearby park you can visit. You might have to work at it a little. Standing outside in the sunshine can help, but this method works best if you can immerse yourself in nature. Walking around a park or sitting by a lake or pond would be best. If you can escape to the mountains or go camping, that would certainly align with the idea of enjoying nature, but those types of trips have higher costs and take way more planning and coordination. I'm referring to more of a quick jolt of nature.

How to Handle New Stress:
The previous section dealt more with ways to lower general, chronic life stress. It's about building enough margin into your life so you can purposefully and effectively deal with the other stresses that pop up. In the heat of the moment, you won't have time to dig out a how-to book and review steps. You'll just have to react.

Assess the Situation: What you should do depends largely on what you're facing. In most cases, seeking more information's a good first step. Questions that may help illuminate the situation:
- Who's affected by the situation?
- How directly are you impacted by the incident?
- Is the situation a one-time thing or a long-term, pervasive problem?
- Does the crisis revolve around you or are you just along for the ride?
- If everything went right, what's the best-case scenario? If everything went wrong, what's the worst-case scenario? These two questions are good for getting a big picture perspective of what's going on.
- What can you do to make the situation better?

Form a Plan of Action: The ugly truth may be that you have very little control over the source of the stress. But there's always something you can do. It might be as simple as taking better care of yourself or younger siblings so your folks can put their time and energy into dealing with the situation. Kindness can be spontaneous, but often, it must be purposeful.

If you're the source ... try to determine if there's a fix. Is the problem related to health or behavior or both? If you're sick, your main job should be getting better. School can wait. Do the best you can to keep up, but if it's having a negative impact on your health, step back. If the source needs medical or psychological attention, then seek it.

If you're not the source ... try to determine if there's a fix. Do you wield any influence over the situation? School's important, but it's only one aspect of your life. Family matters a great deal too.

Identify a perfect solution (whether it's feasible or not): What would fix the problem? More money? A cure? An event never happening? No matter how ridiculous the solution may seem, knowing it can give you some peace of mind.

Implement a small solution: You may not be able to completely fix the problem, but you can likely make it better. Identify the key players and decide how to make their lives better. The small solution might be nothing more than your presence, a hand-written note, a phone call, or a batch of homemade cookies. Don't try to invent a new side to yourself for the situation. Work with your strengths and within your means.

Evaluate the Results: Face every situation like it was the scientific method. After you've identified the problem, you've naturally hypothesized about the source and a possible fix. Your experiment happens when you try your solution on the problem. The next logical step involves evaluating the results. Did your solution help? From there, you make a new decision about how to approach the problem, develop a new possible solution, and implement it. You might be in this phase for a while until you can draw a definitive conclusion about your plan of action.

You're Not Alone:

Family, friends, counselors, doctors, teachers, and preachers can help. Empathy lets one understand and relate to another without having to go through the exact same ordeal. On the flip side, very few things are truly unique. No matter what you're dealing with, somebody somewhere has been there and knows the best way to heal.

The biggest initial hurdle will likely be asking for help. Decide who you can confide in. Sharing your heart isn't going to be easy, but it might be worth it. Understand that many adults are legally bound to take the matter to higher authorities under certain circumstances. That's not meant to scare you. If you need help getting out of a bad situation, most adults will jump at the chance to support you.

Conclusion:

Whether your problems only affect you or touch many lives, they're likely to affect your ability to do the school thing well. Managing everyday stress will let you have the emotional energy to deal with larger issues that surface. Having a plan of action in place before a crisis pops up can help ease you through the tough stuff. Finally, know the people resources that exist around you. The courage to open up has to come from you, but there are usually a lot of people rooting for you.

Chapter 4:
You Reap What You Sow

Introduction:

Almost every piece of information or advice you've gotten thus far could have been compiled by nearly anybody. In this chapter, I'll start earning my keep by sharing classroom insights from a teacher's perspective. The goal is to improve communication between students and teachers. Like it or not, we're in the information business. More than that, teachers exist to expand your knowledge of the world. Will every classroom run the way I describe? No. Will every teacher react the way I predict? Also, no. But for every unique quirk you'll run into, there's also fundamental truths about how to handle people in a way most likely to have favorable outcomes for both parties.

Negative and Positive Attention:

For simplicity's sake, let's assume that there are only two types of attention: negative or positive. Many people can't distinguish between negative and positive attention. To them, any attention is good attention.

The Difference Between Negative and Positive Attention: Negative attention has its roots in something a person does that evokes negative emotions in others. These can range from annoyance to mild disgust to outright anger to darker things like a sense of powerlessness. Positive attention has its roots in something a person does that produces a good shift in the emotions of others.

How to Get Negative Attention: Everybody knows of at least one classmate who gets noticed for all the wrong reasons. Talking non-stop, being rude to fellow classmates, making demands, being rude to the teacher, disrupting class in one of a hundred ways, and bothering other students are some of the many ways to gather negative attention.

Why do People Want Negative Attention? Some people desperately need the approval of others. I want to believe that every child has a charmed homelife, but the sad truth may be that many don't have the emotional support they need from that quarter. The deficit gets filled in other ways. They mistake negative attention for positive attention because certain peers feed into the emotion.

Let's pretend there's a gang of young men desperate to prove themselves to each other. They're throwing stones at a mangy, street cat. The cat is having a royal freakout, which some of the young men find amusing. It's a bad scene, but even if one of the young men feels bad for the cat, he might not speak up for fear of being labeled as a weakling.

One person's negative is another's positive, but for the sake of this book, we're basing negative and positive off the teacher's perspective. You might think that ridiculous, but we're mainly talking about building up goodwill in the class because that's the easiest way to open lines of communication within the classroom.

How to Get Positive Attention: Answering questions, asking powerful, relevant questions, helping your peers, phrasing things as requests, and making a genuine effort to pay attention and participate lead to positive attention. You might fear that some of these activities may earn you a "teacher's pet" label. People do love their labels. You'll eventually reach a point in life where you either change yourself to fit the labels people put on you or you charge forward heedless of their poisonous whispers.

Why You Should Want Positive Attention: Think of positive attention as classroom credit. Build up a reputation as somebody helpful and reliable. That way, when you need something, others will be more inclined to stand up for you. Trust me. At some point, you're going to want something from your teacher. This could be as small as the chance to stretch your legs and as large as moving a test or taking a second look at how a project was graded.

Your reputation will precede you. Make sure you're building a reputation that says you're doing everything you can on your end. Teachers notice which students float along, strive hard, or sail through. Later in life, your teacher will be replaced with a boss who holds your fate—and your paycheck—in his or her hands. The habits you build when you're young tend to stick with you.

Caution: Do not expect that merely following rules earns you favors. This isn't a corrupt quid pro quo (this for that/you give something to get something) system. It's about kindness and understanding. Be the sort of person who helps out when and where and however you can.

Phone Etiquette:

Note: This section may not be relevant for every student because many districts and teachers have specific policies that will supersede these guidelines.

- **Don't hide the phone under a desk.** It's pretty obvious when you're not paying attention and you're staring under your desk. (And the screen's glowing.) Even if your teacher's completely oblivious and you do get away with playing on your phone during the lesson, you're missing out on the learning part and will have to work twice as hard later if you intend to comprehend the lesson.
- **Only use your phone when you're allowed to use your phone.** Ever had somebody mad at you because they think you're ignoring them? Phones are wonderful things, but it's generally rude to ignore somebody in favor of the phone.
- **Only use your phone how you're supposed to use your phone.** There might be times you are asked to use your phone for something related to the lesson of the day. This isn't a great time to check in with every social media site.

- **When asked to put your phone down or away, do so immediately.** This will show that you're capable of listening to instructions and likely earn you goodwill. If the teacher says "put the phone down" he or she probably means "put the phone away." By *away*, I—and your teacher—mean in a location that's not easy to access. The corner of your desk would not qualify. Upside down on the corner of your desk would not qualify. In your pocket would not qualify.
- **Turn off the pinging, vibrating, and flashing parts of your notifications.** It's distracting and likely annoying.
- **Don't use your mom and dad as an excuse for checking your phone constantly.** If there's a specific reason for your parents to be contacting you, then clear it with the teacher ahead of time. The main office of your school probably has a working phone line, and they know your schedule. They can find you if needed. Once upon a time, actually not that ago, not everybody had a miniature computer on their person every hour of the day. You can and will survive without social media for the duration of your class period.
- **Don't claim to need to use the restroom if you're only going to check your phone.** You might actually need to use the restroom later in the class. This has less to do with "getting away with something" and more to do with being honest in all of your dealings with people.
- **Don't claim to need to go to the nurse if you're only going to check your phone.** This comes back to your credibility. Once you build up a reputation as a liar, it's very hard to regain your credibility. This will damage your classroom reputation.
- **If you're not comfortable with turning in your phone when asked to do so, counter with an acceptable alternative.** If you say you're going to put it away, do so, but then have the phone out five seconds to five minutes later because you can't help yourself, you're also destroying your credibility. Once again, *away* should be out of your reach, not in your pocket. A phone addiction might seem like an amusing thing, but if you create bad habits now, it can come back and bite you later in life, like during your first job interview.

What to Do with an Awesome Reputation:

Cherish it. Use it, just don't abuse it. Reputations are tough to build and easy to destroy. A solid reputation as a good student might open certain opportunities for you.

Possible Privileges:
- **Taking a walk:** If you're done your work and need a short break, I see no problem asking to take a walk. This should not be done more than once per class period, and the walk itself should be kept to a modest time, say 2-4 minutes.
- **Filling your water bottle:** You get a walk plus you can grab a drink. Even if it's the beginning of class, as long as you're quick and responsible about it, this shouldn't be an issue. Where you may run into problems is if you make a habit of taking 15-minute walkabouts that include randomly hanging out in other classes just to avoid this one.
- **Having a snack:** I'm a high school chemistry teacher, so eating food in the room is forbidden. Students get exasperated by this, but it really comes down to safety concerns. Spacing being what it is, I'm not the only teacher in a classroom in a given day, and I may or may not know what the other teachers have going on. High school lab chemicals and food don't mix well. Being able to eat a snack in the hallway is a privilege you may lose altogether if you try to sneak food.
- **Going to get food from the cafeteria:** This takes longer than simply consuming a snack you already have with you. A solid reputation will certainly help with this request. If you're in danger of failing the course or have built up a reputation as a lazy student, your chances of scoring a cafeteria run sink. The rare exception is if a teacher irrationally likes you enough or really wants to get rid of you for a few minutes.

  Hold up: Did I just say that a negative reputation might also have some perks? Unfortunately, yes. But don't mistake a privilege earned by being annoying with one granted because you earned it. In these cases, it might open one door while permanently locking another. In other words, there may be unexpected consequences later.

- **Listening to music while you work:** Being able to have a personal playlist going is a privilege, not a right. If you can prove that you can work while listening, great. If you're constantly interrupting yourself to change songs, not so great.
- **Playing video games on your phone or a handheld system:** As a teacher, I have a set agenda of stuff I need to get through and tasks I need you to accomplish. That said, people often work at different paces. If you happen to be a swift worker who's completely mastered the lesson of the day and has not gone out of your way to tick me off, many doors open for you.
- **Reading a book for pleasure or a different class:** Same speech as for video games.
- **Doing homework for another class:** This is a tricky one, especially if you're not doing well in the class you're currently sitting in. Being a student is tough. Hopefully, your teacher understands this. They were all students sometime in the past. This is where having a good class reputation can help. If you've proven that you can handle the workload of the current class, you'll earn the right to switch gears.

Possible Privileges:

Conclusion (and Disclaimer):

Your teacher might be distinctly tougher than I am on these privileges. He or she may be nicer than I am too. The points are merely examples and possibilities. If you don't get to indulge in any of them, don't worry. The solid reputation you're building will pay off in other ways. Also remember, that you're building your character. The only benefit may be that you're less likely to be mistaken for a lazy, good-for-nothin' in the future because you'll be used to putting in honest work.

Chapter 5:
Cultivate Effective Classroom Communication

Introduction:

Miscommunication may be amusing in sitcoms, but when they occur in a classroom, usually only frustration comes of it. First, let's explore the various means of communication. Then, we can focus on purposeful steps to improving communication at all levels. You may be tempted to think the responsibility for clear communication rests solely on your teacher. There's truth to the belief, but it's not the whole truth. Much of the responsibility lies with the teacher, but you too have a part to play.

Classrooms are places of business. Keeping the atmosphere light, clear, and respectful allows for the best communication. Information is being presented or discovered, sometimes both. Busy and lively are good things in a classroom. Chaos is not good.

Ways People Communicate:

Since it could be said that the perspective here matters, I'm going to base the simple definitions of these forms off of you.

Verbally: What you say goes a long way in conveying what you mean. Words spoken aloud are the simplest, most direct form of shuttling messages back and forth. This method depends heavily on your ability to think on your feet. It has the advantage of being short and to the point.

Aurally: This goes hand in hand with verbal communication and has to do with what you absorb as you listen. You may think listening is a passive thing and that you have no choice because you're trapped, but active listening is key to success in school. Active listening takes both attention and effort. It's the opposite of phasing out.

Through Emails: If you need to speak up about a matter that requires deeper thought, you might want to send an email. You could also have a notecard with you so you don't forget something when you go to speak with somebody in person, but usually, if you're putting your points in written form, it's partly because you want the slight emotional barrier.

Body language: Your behavior and demeanor speak volumes more than words can. Behavior refers to what you do, and demeanor has to do with how you carry yourself. Both are likely to be broadcast by your body language.

Tips for Improving Your Classroom Communication:
Most of this advice will boil down to think about what you're doing and be purposeful about how you present yourself, regardless of medium.

Verbally: Choose your words wisely. I'm not demanding you write and rehearse an entire speech every time you need to approach your teacher but consider the implications of the words you go with. Let's take the desire to use the rest room and analyze a few ways it could be phrased:

- **Can I use the restroom?** Technically, I'm guessing this isn't the real question you wish to ask. It implies a question of ability not permission. Still, it's polite enough to pass muster.
- **May I use the restroom?** Your best bet, both polite and straightforward.
- **I've gotta pee.** Direct, but there's no actual question. This is a statement. Your intent is ambiguous, which requires the teacher to ask some follow up questions.
- **I'm going to use the restroom.** The statement is clear and direct, but it carries way more attitude than the question version. Depending on your teacher, this may be fine. Some teachers may not even want you to interrupt the classroom flow anyway. These brave souls trust you know what you're doing and will find your way back. That's likely the way of things in college, but in high school, the burden of care placed on teachers tends to be higher. It's nicer to make sure they know where you're going in case guidance or the front office asks to speak with you.

When in doubt, present your desires as requests. You can't go wrong with genuine politeness and pleasantries. Try to avoid anything that smacks of outright demand. Greetings and farewells may go a long way in improving the atmosphere.

Caution: You may be tempted to think you're in the right and deserve to go wherever you want. Even if that's true, the way you ask can have varying results. I once had a student say, "I'm leaving at 11:00." No context. No more information. He even doubled down and dug in with the attitude when I asked some clarifying questions. Needless to say, he didn't make his meeting.

Aurally: Active listening leads to better understanding. Communication's a two-way street. If you're not understanding the lesson being presented, there's a breakdown in communication. The fault may be because of your teacher, but it can also rest with you. Regardless of fault, you still need to repair the lines so you can successfully navigate the course. Active listening can take a few forms. It could be about keeping your mind alert and focused, taking notes while you listen, or asking clarifying questions.
Take home point: Don't be passive about absorbing information.

Through Emails: If you choose to employ this medium, do so with care. I'll have a longer how-to later about composing emails, but I want to spend this brief time explaining the advantages and disadvantages of this form of communication.

Advantages of Email:
- There's a record of the whole exchange.
- If done well, it shows initiative and responsibility on your part.
- There's flexibility on both sides for when the conversation takes place.
- Writing an email lets you take your time and choose words with more care.
- It's impersonal since you don't have to directly face the person being addressed.

Disadvantages of Email:
- The exchange naturally takes longer.
- Emails can take way longer to compose than holding an actual conversation with a person.
- It's easy to make the wrong assumption if the wording is ambiguous. There's no other context, like expression, to aid with the interpretation.
- Not everybody checks email regularly. (I'm obsessive about checking my email, but that's because I like writing. That makes emails one of my favorite forms of communication.)

Body Language:
You're probably crazy busy with school and extracurricular activities. Nevertheless, try to be aware of your body language. I am not saying you need to go around wearing a creepy smile. In fact, please don't. I'm saying, try to keep your head up. Falling asleep in class might be tempting, but it's also rude. Try to appear alert if you can't feign interest.

You do not need to fold your hands on your desk and act like a good little automaton. Still, you should be aware of your limbs and where you place them. I'm aware that school desks were designed for function, not comfort, but good posture conveys more interest than melting into your seat.

Culture may dictate differently, but American culture's cool with you making eye contact. Even with this point, be cognizant of what your eye contact is conveying. Glaring, gazing, staring, and watching all have different context. Eyes and other facial structures are very expressive. You can broadcast everything from empathy to apathy to hatred to disgust with them. You want the message spilling from them to be either neutral or positive. Even if you disagree with the teacher, you want your body language speaking of intellectual challenge not hostility.

Effective Attitudes (Regardless of Medium):

Whether you're writing an email to a teacher or sitting in the middle of a deadly boring class, you want to be known for several positive traits: honesty, humility, hard work, and authenticity.

Honesty: You may not believe that trust matters in a school setting, but trust always matters. If you didn't do the homework, say so. If you know of a wrong happening, certainly don't take part in it. I am not saying you should divulge specific names, but perhaps the teacher should be aware if there's cheating going on concerning homework or assessments. If you are among the cheaters, realize the error of your ways and change.

Caution: I'm not necessarily saying you must confess to the teacher. You might feel guilty, but if nobody has caught you, there's a good chance that saying something after the fact leads to more trouble. You'll have to weigh the matter for yourself as it happens. Flip side: if something is bothering your conscience, confessing it can clear the air for you.

Humility: Being humble involves not distinctly drawing attention to yourself when you do something right. It may also lead to a willingness to help others without the hope of a reward. Learn the difference between cockiness and confidence. The first term smacks of arrogance. The second term is kind of an unwritten goal of going through high school. Being humble should lead you along the correct path toward confidence.

Hard Work: Understand that there's a difference between staring in the general direction of the textbook for a few hours and actively seeking to comprehend the lesson. You might think: *my teacher stinks at their job, why should I pick up the slack? It's not fair.* And you might be completely correct. But the failure of others doesn't change the mandate to do the best you can in every situation. You're still the one who needs to earn good enough grades to pass high school. Colleges and future bosses won't be able to see the circumstances surrounding the grades you earned.

Authenticity: It's very easy to wear an emotional mask at school. We think "putting on airs" is a thing straight out of regency romance stories, but people do it all the time. If you don't like something, don't pretend otherwise. In other words, try to make the best of the situation, but do not change who you are and how you behave on a whim.

Caution: This should not be taken as a license to be the poster child for the word grumpy just because that's a normal state of being for you. If that's the case, seek a new state of being that's more conducive to being in public.

How to Handle Conflict:

I hate conflict, so I avoid it like a plague. It's not the healthiest way to handle that. You can try avoidance, and sometimes, the method will work for a time. However, avoidance only ignores the issue. It doesn't fix it.

In order to deal with classroom conflict effectively, follow these steps:
1. Identify the source of the conflict.
2. Evaluate the influence you have over the source of the conflict.
3. Seek the counsel of those you trust. Try to avoid turning the telling into a time to complain.
4. Decide whether a direct or indirect approach would be better.
5. If you've chosen a direct method, face the source and implement your plan. If you've chosen an indirect method, set your plans in motion and watch what happens.
6. Evaluate the effectiveness and adjust.

If the cause for the disruption is other people, talk to the teacher and see if he or she can do anything to alleviate the situation. Understand that there might not be an easy fix, depending on how much chaos guidance decided to put in a room together. Nevertheless, it's always good to confirm that the teacher's aware of your concerns. If the conflict is with the teacher, talk to your guidance counselor or another teacher you trust or even your parents.

Conclusion:

You can't control the world. Would be cool, but that's not how life works. The person you have the most influence over is yourself. Keep your attitudes and actions above reproach, so that when you bring up issues, nobody can assume the fault lies with you.

Part 2:
The Practical Portion

Chapter 6:
Learn to Read Your Teacher

Introduction:

Not sure what thought you've ever put into considering who your teacher is outside of school. Probably none and that's fair. Still, basic survival instinct ought to tell you that you should identify the power players in any situation. No matter what the teacher's personality is, he or she will be a power player in the room. By that, I mean this person has the privilege and responsibility for overseeing the things that happen in the classroom. To be blunt, you will have to deal with this person, you might as well walk into the situation as prepared as possible.

Quick Personality Assessment:

Once you've had a chance to meet your new teacher, ask yourself a series of short personality questions based on your observations. You may not be able to answer some of these based on first impressions. Also, these are extremes, so the truth likely belongs somewhere in the middle of them.

Is the teacher ...
- Modest or vain?
- Strict or lenient?

- Set or adaptable?
- Funny or boring?
- Excitable or calm?
- Sincere or sarcastic?
- Formal or informal?
- Stressed or carefree?
- Soft-spoken or loud?
- Fashionable or plain?
- An extrovert or introvert?
- Organized or disorganized?
- Punctual or perpetually late?
- A good oral communicator or a bad oral communicator?
- A good written communicator or a bad written communicator?

Why is this useful?

The more you know, the easier it will be to adjust your behavior to work well with the teacher. Often that will be way easier said than done. Certain personality traits take more patience to endure than others. At the very least, you can approach each day with the proper mental preparation.

I once sat in on a demonstration lesson where the man vying for the job opened by saying, "I'm the greatest teacher ever." He paused a moment then continued, "Look, your teacher hasn't disagreed." He then began his actual lesson. Though I can't be certain how that opening made the students feel, I can tell you the normal classroom teacher did not take kindly to his cocky attitude. Personally, I want to believe that statement was just the man's humor going awry. If such a person becomes your teacher, you have my condolences. Now, let's talk strategy.

Basics of Teacher Wrangling:

You can't go wrong with trying to be likable, but certain strategies are more effective if people agree with you. Picture it like a video game where you have various lines of dialogue and people react to you differently, depending on the alignment of the line. Keep in mind that true Renegade options have real world consequences. So, don't go punching out people for no good reason.

Tips and tricks:

- **Don't complain.** In school and in life, there will be plenty of unpleasant things you're asked to do. School might be boring, difficult, or both. Complaining may be a good temporary release, but it could also irritate the teacher.
- **Be calm but firm.** If the teacher is trying to pick a verbal fight with you, either ignore them or answer softly (as in don't shout) but firmly (as in don't back down). Seek help from a trusted adult.
- **Pick the right battles.** If it comes down to a power struggle, consider letting the teacher win on stupid, irrelevant points. Try to understand the reason behind the power struggle. Finding the source, may help you eliminate the teacher's perceived need to run power trips. Do not seek conflict with the teacher. It might seem like a point of pride to one-up the teacher. Winning in the moment may also feel great, but play the long game. Your teacher is less likely to want to do you any favors or give you the benefit of the doubt if their gut feeling is *this kid is trouble.*
- **Help out where you can.** Earning a bit of goodwill might come in handy. Besides, it's good training on how to be a decent human. You know, open doors for people, lend a neighbor your pen, or be the runner when last-minute copies need to be made. **Aside:** Don't sell pens or pencils to your classmates. While technically business savvy, this makes you seem like an opportunistic jerk willing to take advantage of any situation to make a buck.
- **Ignore or embrace the quirks.** I don't like spiral stuff on papers that get turned in. It's a relatively mild, harmless quirk. If you know your teacher gets annoyed by something specific, take the extra second to deal with it. Little niceties won't make or break a relationship, but they're useful for keeping to someone's good side.
- **Do not go over the teacher's head.** You may have just cause to go to higher authorities, but if you learn nothing else in this entire book, learn this. If you have a problem with the teacher, go directly to them first. They will not appreciate if they're called on something because a student ran immediately to the

vice principal or supervisor. A good vice principal or supervisor will turn you around and make you deal with the teacher anyway in most cases. There are always exceptions to this. If you have cause to believe the teacher's doing something blatantly illegal or they're making you feel extremely uncomfortable, then you may have cause to go to a different adult first.

- **Listen to and follow directions carefully (but don't wing it).** You'd be surprised how rare this one can be. If you missed directions because of a lapse in attention, it's better to risk irritating the teacher than not understand the assignment. In lab situations, it's imperative you have a clear understanding of the procedure before beginning. Making stuff up as you go is dangerous and stupid.

- **Distinguish between critiques and attacks.** Let's say that every time you get a paper back from the teacher it's ripped to shreds. You may feel like the teacher doesn't like you. Maybe he spends the period glaring at you. Try not to take it personally. In this case, he's likely just a grumpy person. As for the part about obliterating your writing skills, that might be his strong interpretation of his job. They don't teach tact and bedside manners in grad school for education. Many people pick up the skill as time moves on, but you could just be lucky enough to be very early or very late in somebody's career. If one gets too comfortable, they can stop caring about sugarcoating corrections.

- **Be genuine but try to find common interests.** If you know your teacher is a diehard fan of a certain sports team, search up some weekend game scores. If you happen to like the same team, commiserate if your team lost and congratulate if the team won. That sort of thing. If you know your teacher saw the same movie you did, ask him or her for movie thoughts and reactions.

- **Be polite and courteous but don't overdo it.** Being nice should be your normal, default mode as a human, but if you're overly solicitous, people may think you have an ulterior motive.

Advanced Teacher Wrangling - Adaptation:

As in a video game, adjusting what you say and how you act can help you navigate the tricky business of understanding your teacher. If you can read the person, you will have an easier time learning from them.

What the quick personality quiz means for them (and you):

- **Modest or vain?** The way people approach life can be most readily seen by the way they present themselves, but this goes beyond how they dress and what kinds of accessories they have. Either personality can be approachable. The difference would likely be in how you relate to them.

- **Strict or lenient?** If the teacher is strict, you'll have to concentrate on handling your workload well due to the lower chance of catching a break if you need more time on something. If the teacher has a reputation for being lenient, you have a bit more breathing space. Feel free to avail yourself of that privilege, but don't abuse the system because even lenient teachers draw lines on acceptable behavior.
- **Funny or boring?** Humorous people are more entertaining. Every subject will have portions you're not particularly fond of. Whether your teacher can keep you entertained in class or not, this just determines how hard you'll have to fight to stay alert. You should always seek to get adequate rest at night.
- **Excitable or calm?** Have you ever met somebody who reminds you of a caffeinated squirrel? This question deals with relatability. Neither option is better than the other. They are merely different. Excitable people may be more apt to entertain you as you learn. Calm people may be easier to talk to one on one. Your best bet in both situations is to engage with the lesson.
- **Formal or informal?** No matter what your teacher's disposition happens to be, you should keep individual interactions more towards the formal side at least in the beginning. As time goes on and you get to know each other, formality can be eased, but the difference in your circumstances should require there to be some degree of formality.

  Aside: Can teachers and students be friends? Yes, but not when the current arrangement is teacher and student. One of my good friends happens to have been my student, but that time was many years in the past. She's an adult now. In turn, I am friends with one of my former teachers and have been for years. Crossing lines of formality while you're still teacher and student leads to trouble.
- **Serious or sarcastic?** Sarcastic people can be hilarious, but sarcasm can be hard to land without hurting feelings. If you discover that your teacher has a penchant for sarcasm, take their comments in stride. Keep things as light as possible. If your teacher's personality falls more towards the serious side,

be direct with your questions. I'm not saying serious people are anti-fun, but they do tend to have a dim view of fooling around. Try to keep a hold on your wild side if that's the case.

- **Stressed or carefree?** If your teacher is stressed, try to keep your interactions brief and light. You do not want to add to the stress. Also, the strain may cause the teacher to not be in the best of moods. When you can catch him or her in carefree moments, take the time to get to know them better. Building up a friendly relationship may brighten their week and ease the stressful days.

- **Soft-spoken or loud?** Again, there's no right or wrong, only a difference in personality. Soft-spoken people usually think deeper about their responses. Boisterous people are more apt to give you a quick answer. Try matching your demeanor to the situation. If your teacher is quiet and contemplative, approach them calmly and rationally. If the teacher is super high energy, be enthusiastic.

- **Fashionable or plain?** This is a simple observation that can give you insight into the teacher's character. Where people spend their time, money, and effort can tell you what they value. The information may not even be useful to you in the moment. If you like a piece of jewelry your teacher is wearing, make a point to compliment him or her. Don't make a scene. Keep it simple. If you've worked hard on an outfit and your teacher notices, awesome. If she's oblivious, don't get insulted.

- **An extrovert or introvert?** Extroverted people thrive by being around others. Introverts get drained by interacting with people. Have you ever seen anybody constantly perky? It's frightening. I'm an introvert. If you have an expansive personality, be aware that others might find that intimidating. On the flip side, if your teacher has a huge personality, don't be intimidated.

- **Organized or disorganized?** Organized people have their ducks in a row. Disorganized people aren't always sure how many ducks they should be chasing down. The teaching profession has greater appeal for people with organized personalities, but there's no set rule about that. The only advantage or disadvantage I can see for you is how organized you must be if you need to approach the teacher about a specific matter. It can be terribly frustrating if your teacher loses a paper or a test you wish to talk about but keep your cool. Be persistent yet polite about asking about the misplaced item.

- **Punctual or perpetually late?** This question has more to do with what you can get away with than the others. If your teacher's always late, you have an extra few seconds to get to class yourself. If your teacher values punctuality, put some hustle into your steps. Sometimes, the scheduling minions— also known as guidance counselors—let cold-hearted computers generate your schedule.

   Translation: it may not be humanly possible to get from class to class without sprinting. Explain the problem to your teacher and do your best to make it on time.

   Note: Attitude matters. If a student is a few seconds late but clearly tried to be on time, I'm more prone to excuse it occasionally. However, if a student casually strolls in two minutes late every single day, they're going to get marked absent every time.

- **Set in their ways or adaptable?** At the risk of sounding ageist, older teachers have a lot more experience to draw from and therefore can find it harder to embrace the latest and greatest electronic technology. The same principle holds true in other aspects. Technology happens to be the easiest and most obvious example. Both types of teachers need love and understanding. Those who prefer old-school methods of teaching avoid technology. Those who love technology can be annoying because they're always changing things up on you. Both will require patience from you.

- **A good oral communicator or a bad oral communicator?** Teachers usually excel at oral communication. It takes a special kind of crazy to work in a classroom if you don't like public speaking. But ease with something doesn't always translate to clear and understandable. If you're having a hard time understanding what the teacher's saying, try asking the question through an email. If you need something repeated a lot before you can understand it, see if you can get permission to record the instructional portions of class.

- **A good written communicator or a bad written communicator?** Bad communication in written form doesn't necessarily have to mean difficult to comprehend. It could also mean: *never checks emails*. Go to see the teacher in person if that's the case. You may have to be purposeful about changing your schedule to accommodate this.

Worst-case Scenarios:

What do you do if your teacher turns out to be a tyrant or an arrogant jerk or just an incompetent hot mess?

Dealing with the Tyrant: First things first. Tyrants are nothing more than titled bullies. Unfortunately, they exist in every arena of life. They live and breathe for power and control. Without becoming a sycophant who mindlessly says yes to everything the tyrant demands, try to stay on his or her good side. Confrontation rarely goes over well with these sorts. They expect conflict. I suspect they even relish it. The best thing you can do is pick and choose the right battles or fly under the radar. I am not saying to roll over and play dead, though there may be moments where that's a valid self-preservation tactic. Try not to needlessly antagonize this type of teacher, tempting though that might be. Also, if possible, try to rein in classmates inclined to provoke the teacher.

Aside: Some sadistic students enjoy provoking the teacher. If you have any social influence, do your best to quash their tendencies. If the teacher's not happy, the entire mood of the class can shift to negative. No classroom should stuck in an us vs. them mentality.

Accept that you may not be able to completely change your teacher. At the same time, never underestimate the positive power of respect and kindness. Does this type of teacher deserve your respect? To the extent that every human does, yes. Is it right or fair that they have power over you? Not really, but you are master over your emotions and actions, not theirs. Your job is to gain the most from the class despite the lousy circumstances.

Dealing with the Arrogant Jerk: Some people believe the world revolves around them. This attitude leads to some unpleasant personality traits, like arrogance. My advice: stick to the business at hand. The silver lining of self-absorption is that such people tend to be too busy admiring themselves to bother with others. That could mean you're on your own for learning the subject, but if you stick to a policy of *ignore the teacher's shenanigans*, the class itself should run fine. If you avoid overtly challenging this type of teacher, you should be fine. Stay off their radar.

Dealing with the Incompetent Hot Mess: Brilliant people know their subject inside and out. They push the boundaries of the known and make awesome breakthroughs. They're also usually lousy teachers because there's a disconnect between their brains and the language needed to reach the rest of us mere mortals. (Of course, there are exceptions: geniuses who turn out to be excellent teachers.) Once again, you might have to conquer the subject on your own or find other ways to bridge the information gap. Like the Arrogant Jerk, the Incompetent Hot Mess can be relatively harmless when it comes to interpersonal actions.

You might even be able to help this type of teacher by doing little things to keep him or her organized. The good news to this type of person is that they genuinely love the subject and want to help you access the information. Watching videos, getting a tutor, asking friends who are doing well in the subject, or some combination thereof can help you overcome the teacher's shortcomings.

Conclusion:

Most teachers won't hit any of the worst-case scenarios. Accurately reading your teacher's personality will make it easier to approach him or her. It might also give you the edge you need to unravel the mystery of their teaching style. The better you understand the person, the easier it will be to learn from them.

Chapter 7:
Choosing Battles

Introduction:

There's naturally going to be some overlap between several chapters of this book. Improving your people skills to the point where you can always get your way might be ideal, but for the normal people, here are some insights into picking the right battles.

The Teacher's Not (Always) the Enemy:

I will concede that some of the topics to come may make it seem as if the teacher's the enemy. For most situations, this is not the case. In the vast majority of cases that pop up, the teacher's a neutral party or even an ally.

Situations Where the Teacher is an Ally:

For now, I'll keep this section brief. Next chapter, I'll expand on how to approach these situations.

Extra Help: Teachers have a vested interest in their students' success. While the timing of extra help may be something worth discussing, you should find your teacher quite willing to offer you help outside of the normal class period.

Recommendations: First jobs and future colleges likely want to hear how you handle yourself. Thus, they'll seek a recommendation letter from a teacher. As long as you're halfway decent about choosing whom to ask to write this letter, you should be fine.

Potentially Contentious Situations (and How to Handle Them):

Three broad categories have the potential to cast the teacher in either neutral or enemy light. This chapter will focus on the question of whether to enter the battle or not. Next chapter will deal with more specifics about how to ask questions properly, but I'll explore some of that now.

Tardies to Class: If you find yourself being perpetually late to class, stop and examine the situation before deciding whether to approach the teacher or not. Why are you late? How late are you? How often are you late? What is your relationship with the teacher? The answers to those questions should give you the information to make a wise decision.

- **Enter the battle if ...** you have a valid reason for being late, aren't late by much, aren't late too often, and/or have a decent relationship with the teacher. Please note that you do not need every single question to be answered favorably to make it worth entering the battle. If you have a valid reason for being tardy, that alone may be enough.

ENTER
the battle

Aren't late too often	Aren't late by much
Have a decent relationship with the teacher	Have a valid reason for being late

- **Do not enter the battle if ...** you're late for personal reasons. These include but aren't limited to: having to walk a boyfriend/girlfriend to a different class, always helping an injured friend get to class, needing to buy a snack, and just walking slowly. Please don't take this as you shouldn't be nice to people. If there's absolutely no other choice but for you to always walk a person to class due to an injury, get a pass.

DO NOT ENTER
the battle

Walking a boyfriend/girlfriend to a different class	Walking slowly
Helping an injured friend get to class	Needing to buy a snack

Extensions: Time is a precious thing. When you find yourself needing more to accomplish the task you've been presented with, consider a few things before broaching the topic. Why do you need an extension on the test or assignment? Will an extension actually improve your performance on the test or assignment? How much is the task worth?

- **Enter the battle if ...** the assignment is worth a lot, an extension will help, and you have a reasonable excuse for needing it. Life definitely gets in the way of school and vice versa. If something comes up and throws you for a loop, ask your teacher for an extension. Expect probing questions. You are not obligated to spill the entire situation to your teacher, but be aware that he or she would be remiss in their duties of care if they didn't look into your reasons for needing an extension.

  Occasionally, the guidance department gives the faculty a head's up on special circumstances, but until you know otherwise, your safest assumption is that the teacher knows nothing. If you had to visit a parent, sibling, grandparent, or close friend in the hospital the night before a big surgery, that's a whole different situation. Same goes for if you were in the hospital the night before. Ask away.

- **Do not enter the battle if ...** the penalty for handing in the assignment late won't significantly affect the overall grade or the extension won't really improve your performance. The validity of the reason you require an extension will be affected by many variables. Only you can make that decision. If you chose to stay out late the night before a big test, you probably shouldn't ask for an extension.
- **Things to consider with extensions:**
    - o How long of an extension are you looking for? Some students would be gold medalists if test avoidance became an Olympic sport. If circumstances require you to need some extra study time, that's fine. However, the longer you put off making up a test, the harder it is to keep up with the class. You'll be juggling old material and new information. I don't have hard statistics, but I can safely say that students tend to do worse on tests if they don't take it with their classmates.
    - o Group projects are harder to get extensions for because others may depend on you to complete a certain portion by a given deadline. The best thing you can do is communicate with your partners and the teacher. If necessary, ask the teacher to intervene.
    - o You may be asked to complete a different task or test than your peers. Tempting as it may be to think this possibility unfair, consider the need to curb attempts to cheat. In the case of a group project, if you're removed from your group, you'll likely have to do an alternative assignment on your own. This isn't about penalizing you for asking for an extension, it's about giving you something with a more flexible timeline. Group projects are by design meant to be able to divide the work. They're not always easy to modify for someone going solo.

Exemptions: If there's any one category of requests to think twice about, it's this. It's best to let the teacher's discretion reign here. If you choose to ask for an exemption from an assignment, be mindful of the pitfalls as you bring forth your request. You should avoid implying that the assignment has little to no worth. (You may be correct in judging its worth as nothing, but it's also about the swiftest way to irritate the teacher.)

Assignments and Grades: I saved the best for last. As the currency most schools run on, grades can lead to cries of joy or despair. As such, people get highly touchy over them.

- **Test Points:** If you're convinced the teacher marked something wrong, certainly bring it up. Attitude still matters. Approach with more of a *I think I was right here* or *hey, could this have been a mistake* attitude rather than a *you're wrong*.
- **Test Knowledge:** If you wish to know why something was marked as incorrect for the sheer purpose of self-improvement, ask. (Hey, I can dream.)
- **Test Content/ Wording:** If the wording of a test tripped you up, seek clarification. You should have sought clarification before the test was handed in, marked, and returned, but since the teacher probably wrote the other tests too, it's best to get a handle on how he or she asks questions.
- **Test Unfairness (Content):** If you think there's a discrepancy between the content taught in the class and the material that shows up on the test, it may be worth discussing with the teacher.
  Warning: Approach with caution. The fact that you're questioning something the teacher put a lot of work into will almost guarantee that he or she starts the discussion on the defensive.
- **Test Unfairness (Partial Credit Distribution):** Even within math and science, there's a lot of partial credit involved in grading. If you think your teacher graded something unfairly, tread with care but feel free to inquire about it. Choosing the right battles in this category is going to be important. Consider that for every time you've gotten the short end of the credit/no credit question, you've also been granted the benefit of the

doubt in a different case. Sometimes, it's to your advantage not to have the teacher take a second look. **Warning:** If you mention that your friend received full credit for the same answer there's a chance that the teacher also revisits the points awarded to your friend. People's policies on partial credit vary widely, and it is possible that the argument hurts your friend's grade more than it helps your grade.

- **End of Quarter/Semester Grade Changes:** This is a wild card that largely depends on what kind of teacher you've drawn in the random lottery of fate. Things to consider: how close are you to that target grade, how hard have you worked, why are you waiting until the end of the marking period to be concerned about your grades? If you do not have reasonable or darn good reasons to those questions, don't bother. If you're .01 away from that A and you have a solid relationship with your teacher, maybe bother.

- **Additional Comments about Grade Changes:** It must be doable. Unless the teacher has zero regard for the grading system, there are limitations to how far he or she can influence the grade at the end of a quarter. If you're missing a ton of work, that's an easy fix. Hand in the work and the grade goes up. If you've done every assignment possible yet still fall a tad short, ask the question, but be prepared for it to go either way. Even if the teacher chooses to take a second look at your grades, it may not be possible to boost it enough to reach your target grade.

You Don't Have to Approach Alone:

The teacher isn't your enemy. In fact, in most situations above, you need to make them your ally as quickly as possible. If you're still intimidated by the thought of approaching your teacher by yourself, bring a friend. Your friend shouldn't be given the same access to your grades as you, but there's nothing wrong with being in the same room to witness the conversation from afar.

When You Should Involve Your Parents:

First contact should be with the teacher either alone or with a friend. Parents can be a wonderful support system, but they may not understand the intricacies of the question you're asking. Teachers can get cagey when parents become involved. Also, by the time you reach high school (and certainly by college), you should begin advocating for yourself.

Not Right Away: Parental involvement can turn a mole hill into a mountain quicker than you can text somebody a smiley face. Once upon a time, I had a parent question the way I graded a quiz. She wrote a massive email that boiled down to I should give her son full credit for his answer. I'd given him half credit. The question involved marking things true or false and fixing false statements so they became true. The student had correctly identified one question as false but provided an invalid fix for it. Luckily, the supervisor I had at the time knew the content well enough to back me up. Moreover, he took the time to write the mother back explaining in great detail why the way I grade the quiz was valid. Ultimately, nothing came of the inquiry, but dealing with it wasted at least a few hours of my time and my supervisor's time. **My point:** parental involvement should not be your first instinct.

The Right Time to Pull the Parent Card: If you've taken the first steps and still have a problem, then consider asking your parents to contact the teacher. Do so with caution. Explain the situation as thoroughly and impartially as possible. Your folks will almost always be 130% on your side, so try not to make the situation an us vs. them thing if it doesn't have to be.

Conclusion:

Grades might be important, but real learning matters more. In a few years, you'll be embroiled in a new set of successes and problems. You may not remember the kinds of trials you faced in high school, but work to hone a good instinct for choosing which battles to wage and which to release. That skill will serve you for the rest of your life.

Chapter 8:
The Art of Asking

Introduction:

Have you considered how many ways there are to state the idea of making a proposal and getting a desirable response? You could be demanding, pleading, or simply asking. Each of these words and phrases has slightly different context. Demanding has a negative connotation. Pleading comes across as desperate, but simply asking might not be forceful enough to convey the importance of your request. Allow me to at least start you on the long journey to understanding the art of asking.

At some point, you're going to want something from somebody. It's best to present the request in a clear, concise manner that will cater to the other person's preference. By that, I mean some people prefer to be dealt with directly and others like having a paper trail. Regardless of medium though, there are things you should do and things to avoid doing.

What Kinds of Requests Does this Cover?

Student requests generally fall into three categories: extensions, grades, and recommendations.

Extensions: Countless reasons exist for needing an extension on a test, paper, or other graded assignment. These reasons range from you simply had poor time management to you got overwhelmed and shut down to you had a family emergency. Life happens. Usually, teachers understand and are willing to grant you an extension. However, the situational circumstances and your reputation may also be weighed in the decision-making process. Sometimes, you will get your extension at a slight penalty to the grade.

Grades: Most requests having to do with grades deal with grade changes. At times, you're 100% in the right because the teacher made a mistake in grading. Other times, you're asking for clarification. Still other times, you're throwing yourself on their mercy to see if you can get a miracle to boost your grade to a certain score.

I'm always surprised by the number of students who really want to do extra credit to bring up their grades when they didn't bother doing the work originally assigned. In those cases, you're probably doomed from the start.

Recommendations: Colleges, internships, scholarships, and even some beginning jobs require a certain number of teacher recommendations. When deciding which teachers to approach, you may want to consider how you performed in his or her class, relevancy to the program, your relationship with the teacher, and his or her workload.

It's (Almost Always) All About Attitude:
Regardless of the delivery method, the way you present yourself and your request will go a long way in determining how it is received. You want to show initiative, but you do not want to come across as demanding.

Make your request a question not a statement: "I'm going to the restroom" is a statement. "May I use the restroom?" is a question. There's a small but powerful difference between them. One borders on a demand, while the other leaves room for the other person to respond.

Very rarely will a teacher deny a request to use the restroom. And definitely don't go around telling teachers it's illegal for them to deny a request to use the restroom. It makes you sound like a pompous jerk. That is not the way to make friends or earn respect. Occasionally, a teacher may ask you if you can wait a moment because they're about to explain something important. If it's an emergency, then say so. They're very rarely going to argue with you.

Make sure your request is legitimate:
Asking to use the restroom to take a walk is generally not a good idea. If you want to take a walk, then make that your request. If you want to use the restroom, get a drink, and take a walk, make that the actual request. Otherwise, you'll likely take far longer expected and have the teacher ready to send out a search party for you.

Take Home Point: You want to come across as sincere and straightforward.

What Isn't About Attitude is About Timing:
Learning when to ask a question will be almost as vital as learning how to ask a question.

Questions About a Test Grade: Straightforward things like multiple choice questions should probably be taken care of right away, but I recommend a 24-hour waiting period before approaching a teacher about correcting the grade for an open-ended/short answer or essay test question. Many students wish to get it sorted in the first two seconds of learning of the possible mistake or inquiring about why they lost so many points on a question. Some teachers may prefer this too, so know if that's the case with your teacher.

I don't recommend handling the issue right away because you're usually upset and high strung. This could lead you to be agitated when making the request. First, agitated people aren't at their peak coherency level. Second, if you're requesting the teacher take another look at your test specifically, the middle of a class isn't the best moment. The teacher will likely be distracted and not be devoting their full attention to the request.

On the flip side, you don't want to wait two weeks to present your request for a grade change. As teachers, we like to think it's about the learning, not just about the grade. If you wait until a marking period closes and then want to turn something in so you don't have a zero that brings your grade down, you better hope you catch your teacher in a very good mood.

Questions About a Letter of Recommendation: Before school, after school, and sometimes lunchtime are the best times for approaching about non-class related issues. Likely, if you're asking for a letter of recommendation from a teacher, they are not your current teacher. Having the common courtesy not to interrupt them will make a good impression.

Two Scenarios Inspired by Real Events:
Scenario 1: A student a teacher had a few years ago gave her a present around Christmas time. Two weeks later, the student asked for a college recommendation.

Result: Student got his recommendation, but the teacher felt manipulated.

GIFT SCENERIO

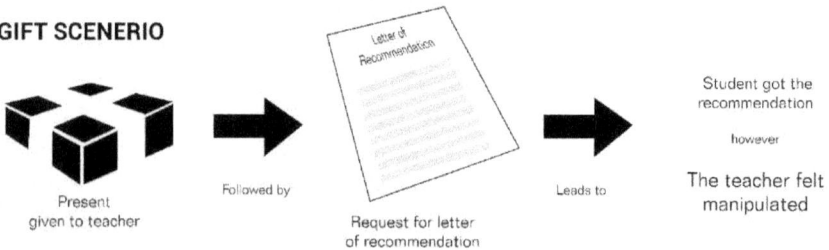

Present given to teacher — Followed by — Letter of Recommendation / Request for letter of recommendation — Leads to — Student got the recommendation however The teacher felt manipulated

Analysis: Neither giving the gift nor asking for a recommendation were wrong per se, but the order of operations made the situation a hair shadier than it needed to be. By giving the gift first, there's an implication of *you owe me one.*

Quick Fix: If the student had asked for a recommendation, gotten it, and then given a gift to the teacher, she would not have felt manipulated. More on giving gifts later.

QUICK FIX

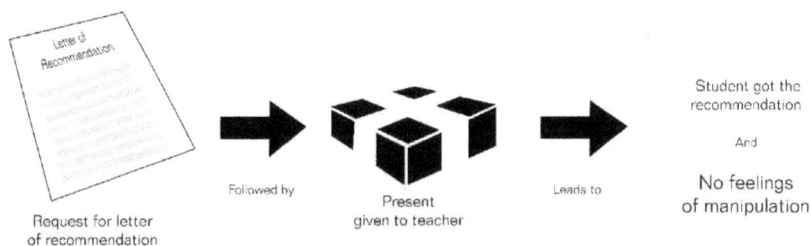

Request for letter of recommendation → Followed by → Present given to teacher → Leads to → Student got the recommendation And No feelings of manipulation

Scenario 2: A student hounded a teacher for a meeting to share about a cool summer experience. At the end of the meeting, the student told the teacher she was applying to a computer science scholarship and asked her for a letter of recommendation.

Result: Student got her recommendation, but this teacher legitimately could not answer some of the questions on the form. Her class had nothing to do with computer coding, so she had nothing to base an assessment of the student's skills on.

Analysis: The student probably should have asked a computer teacher, but that may not have been an option. If she had her heart set on a recommendation from this teacher, she still should have approached the question differently.

Quick Fix: Even just being completely open about the request from the beginning would have helped. Write an email explaining a bit about the summer program, the scholarship, and end the email with a request for a recommendation. Then, follow up in person with the teacher and maybe then expand the information about the neat summer experience.

How to Ask for a College Recommendation Letter:

Start in person. This isn't a rule set in concrete, just a suggestion. When it comes to college recommendations, you may be asking a teacher who has not had you for a few years. No offense, but the teacher might not even remember your name if enough time has elapsed. A quick, in-person request is good form.

Follow any specific instructions the teacher gives you once you've secured their verbal agreement to write you a recommendation. Next step could vary per school, but most will have you fill out a form that lets the teacher know what you're interested in pursuing. You can include your extra curriculars here, but mostly, you want to focus on what you liked and found challenging about the course whose teacher you're getting the recommendation. How did you positively enhance the learning environment of the classroom? If you can honestly say that you asked thoughtful questions or helped your peers, a gentle reminder to that effect would be appropriate. If there's no set place for you to upload this form, you should email the document to the teacher.

Follow up in person or keep in touch by email to let the teacher know of relevant deadlines and results. It's a nice touch if you reach out and thank them once you know what your next step will be. There's no need to give a gift unless you really want to give a tangible gesture of thanks. A note or email would suffice. It's not about the gift, it's about the thought and communication.

More on giving gifts: By their nature, gifts should be unexpected, thoughtful gestures. Teachers work hard. That's the job. In high school, the learning gets broken down into subject areas, so you have quite a few teachers. Nobody expects you and your family to shell out upwards of a hundred dollars or more to give each teacher a gift. If you feel like one teacher went above and beyond and want to show your appreciation, it's perfectly acceptable to give them a gift. It should never be about the monetary value. Even a heartfelt personal note can be a great gift. Understand that gifts are freely given with no expectation of getting something in return. (That's called a bribe and is highly frowned upon in society.) Therefore, your timing on giving a gift matters a great deal.

Conclusion:

Teachers are human. There will be good days and bad days. If it looks like you've caught the teacher at a bad time, come back at a future time. You shouldn't wait until the last minute anyway, so there should be time to reschedule. It might be inconvenient, but that's a small price to pay for making a better impression when you're asking for something. On the flip side, if you have a strong enough relationship with the teacher, maybe getting to see you will be a highlight for them and you can cheer them up. Read the situation and adjust accordingly.

Chapter 9:
Skills for Navigating School and Life

Introduction:

You can't control everything, but most of the time, you don't give yourself enough credit. Tons of vital life skills are not glamorous. As hinted at before, many school lessons with later life applications have little to do with the material you're learning in a class.

What are these Vital Life Skills?

Dealing with Pressure and Learning Your Limits: The quest for success can lead people to do crazy things. Students get really stressed out over tests, quizzes, and projects piled on top of social pressures to fit in. Learn to see the big picture. I'm not saying you should give schoolwork a half-hearted effort. Do your level best without damaging your health. Failing a test won't end your world. Acing a test doesn't define you. Try not to worry what other people think of you. Best foot forward and all, but in the end, the opinions of most others matters little in the grand scheme of your life. You may not even keep in touch with most of your classmates after you graduate.

School, Life Skills

Understanding the need to master these vital skills will help navigating through the waters of highschool and beyond, into adult life.

Dealing with Pressure and Learning Your Limits	Reading
Comprehend and Follow Directions	Levels of Writing
When and How to Ask for Help	Time Management
Working with Others	Being Responsible
Identifying Power Players	Advocating for Yourself
Self-Control	

Reading: This one comes easier for some people. Many indulge in it for fun. The ability to read will open many doors for you. The more you practice, the easier it will become. You may not enjoy it because it's difficult due to dyslexia or difficulties concentrating, but this one is worthwhile. By the time you're in high school, I can almost guarantee you take the ability to read for granted. Your parents may have taught you how to read before you even stepped foot in a school, but school can still help you grow in that skill.

Key benefit: You have access to a ton of information.

Levels of Writing: While reading lets you take in vast amounts of information, writing lets you express yourself. Distinguishing between situations where you should be formal and informal will be important both in high school and later in life. You should realize that how you write a text message and how you compose an email involve two different levels of formality. Likewise, writing a reaction paper to a video and writing a research paper for English class will be two different things.

Comprehend and Follow Directions: Whether instructions are given verbally or in written form, you're going to need to comprehend and follow them to accomplish your assignment. Instructions aren't always clear. Sometimes understanding instructions involves quite a bit of interpretation. The ability to take in directions and execute them properly will serve you well in many arenas of life. For example, the instruction to take out the garbage or clean your room might not be interesting but following the direction will help keep your household running smoothly.

When and How to Ask for Help: There's a time to ask for help and a time not to ask for help. Likewise, there's a proper way to ask for help. During the middle of a test is not the proper time to ask for help from your teacher or a fellow student. There's a big difference between asking for clarification and asking for the answer.

Learning how to ask for help is key. Most students will think that point almost too obvious to include here. But by far, this is the one area most students fall completely short.

Very typical extra help conversation:
Student: I'm so confused.
Teacher: Okay. What are you confused on?
Student: Everything.

The above conversation makes it extremely difficult for the teacher to give the student the proper help since most of the time will be spent pinpointing the students' problem.

Time Management: Time might be the most underappreciated gift we have. Choosing how you spend it will define who you are and what others think about you. Do you spend an extra few hours studying or hanging out with friends? In truth, sometimes the right answer will be the studying and sometimes the right answer will be friends. The key to getting the most out of this one is learning to accomplish the obligations efficiently so you have more time to invest in people. Work in enough down time to keep your mind sharp and your relationships strong.

Self-Control: Things don't always work out in your favor. Dealing with disappointment comes with the territory of growing up. Babies cry. Toddlers kick and scream. Even elementary school students throw unholy tantrums. By the time you reach middle and high school, you should be well-versed in controlling the urge to kick and scream. Find a way to dissipate or channel your frustration in productive ways.

Working with Others: I would much rather rely solely on myself, but humans don't always have that luxury. School's the safest place to learn how to work productively with others, whether you get along with them or not. I have a strong dislike for group projects, but I will admit they have some merit. Become the type of person everybody's happy to work with. Try to avoid building a reputation for not being reliable during group projects. If something comes up suddenly that prevents you from fulfilling your part, do your best to communicate well with your groupmates and your teacher.

Being Responsible: Everybody wants to be trusted, but it's something built over time. People rarely wake up one morning and decide to suddenly become responsible. You keep track of little things and work your way up to handling bigger responsibilities. Keeping track of your pens, pencils, calculators, homework, project materials, and other school paraphernalia is just the starting point of being responsible.

How do you build responsibility? Little things like showing up for class on time, being prepared for class, and being aware of your surroundings add up to helping you be more responsible. Always needing to borrow a pen or pencil might seem like a minor point. However, it's also a sign of a deeper underlying issue. This issue could be a lack of money or it could be a character flaw like irresponsibility. If you can't be trusted to keep track of something small like a pen, why should anybody trust you with things of higher importance?

Identifying Power Players: I'm going to define power players here as the people who can affect the classroom. This can be anybody from the teacher to the smartest student to the loudest student to the most obnoxious student. If you can pick out who to align yourself with and who to avoid like a plague, it will make your time in that classroom more tolerable.

Advocating for Yourself (Without Coming Across as a Jerk): Defending yourself may be necessary from time to time. School's a good place to practice advocating for yourself. How you present your case depends largely on the point you must make.

Putting Things in Your Own Words: Plagiarism is essentially passing off somebody else's work as your own. Some teachers use programs to try and catch cheaters who copy and paste whole sections from various websites. These programs aren't foolproof. They can also make mistakes. If you want to check a section yourself, copy and paste it into a search engine and see what results you get. Putting things in your own words will be a vital skill both now and later in life. Besides, if you can accurately keep a point and use different words, you likely understand the point being made.

Advocating Tips:
- Be firm and clear.
- Try to keep emotion out of it. That's a tough thing to ask, but emotion makes things messier.
- Be prepared. If possible, try to anticipate points the other person will raise.
- Listen to the other side. Try not to interrupt the other person if they're making a point. If they're interrupting you, make it clear you don't appreciate that, but keep a hold on your temper too.
- Accept either outcome and roll the experience into your next round of taking a stand.

Cheaters (Almost) Never Prosper:

Several things could happen if you cheat.

You could…

A) Get off scot-free

B) Wind up with a guilty conscience

C) Get a 0 on the assignment

D) Automatically fail the course

Whether you get caught or not, cheating doesn't help you learn. It may also teach you a bad lesson: that the easy way works. Honestly, cheating in high school isn't going to make or break you. However, if you get comfortable with it, you might find yourself doing it later in life and that could have far-reaching consequences. Most white-collar crimes are prompted by a combination of greed and stupidity. What do you think breeds this lovely combination? A mindset comfortable with taking the dishonest, easy way.

Special Note on Plagiarism: Can you get away with it? Sometimes. There are even undetectable forms like hiring somebody to write a paper for you. The ability to *get away with* something should not be your guideline on the morality of the issue. Writing a research paper may be painful, but it's still a skill you will need if you plan to go on to higher levels of academia.

Conclusion:

I hope you like school, but even if you hate it, try to learn from it. I'm not strictly speaking of the academic lessons being presented, though do your best in that area too. Every experience you have in life has the potential to shape something about your character. Use school as a training ground to absorb and cultivate the vital life skills that will serve you well later.

Part 3:
How to Get Help

Disclaimer: If you've read 5 Steps to Surviving Chemistry much of this advice will be very familiar. I'm rewriting it for this book, but most of the ideas have stayed the same.

Chapter 10:
Seeking Help and Wading Through Information

Introduction:

I teach high school chemistry. We had the internet when I was in school, but Google was just becoming a household word. Regardless of subject, if you have a question, there's likely an answer out there on the internet. Be careful, for every right answer there's also a few wrong or misleading ones. Knowing when and how to seek extra help and how to supplement classroom information with internet articles and videos will help you navigate the intricacies of the modern high school curriculum.

Resources Available to Students:

- Your teacher
- Paid tutor or nonpaid tutor
- Class notes, worksheets, and homework
- Your textbook or online textbook
- The internet: websites
- The internet: YouTube and other video tutorials

Resources Available to Students (Annotated):

Your teacher: Believe it or not, this person is your best source for information. He or she makes or at least arranges and formats the tests, quizzes, and other assignments. As such, this person has insider information on what you should concentrate on when you study and can offer excellent tips on how to approach any necessary research. Depending on your relationship with the teacher, he or she may even be willing to help you wade through some of the online resources.

Many times, there are several ways to approach something. For example, in Chemistry, the math can be done through something called the conversion factor method. There may be applications for something called proportions too. I love the first method and despise the second. Thus, I do not teach the second method. The other thing I emphasize is units. I believe that most Chemistry math problems can be successfully navigated if one has a handle on the units. Your teacher may choose to emphasize something else.

To some extent, you will have to adjust how you approach a task to your teacher's method for doing things. That notion may annoy some of you who would argue that there are multiple ways to approach many problems. While true, keep in mind that your teacher has to grade you somehow. If you try a new method with only mediocre success, you risk not being able to get partial credit due to your teacher's inability to follow your work.

Email might be my favorite form of communication, but it certainly has its limitations. While it's excellent for setting up a meeting. It's usually best to seek help in person. Most schools have a policy on extra help, that is help available to the students from the teacher outside of normal school hours. Some places, there are formal office hours, but often, it's up to the individual teacher to decide when and how to offer additional assistance to students. This information ought to be available to you from the teacher's website, but when it doubt, ask the teacher directly.

How do you get the most out of extra help?

- **Make an appointment.** That might seem obvious, and I doubt a teacher would turn you away simply because you failed to make an appointment. However, teachers are busy people. They're not always the easiest to track down. Appointments cut down on the time wasted looking for the teacher.
  Note: Do your best to make any appointments you set up. Sometimes, I think students don't really want to find the teacher.
- **Come prepared.** Try homework or textbook problems on your own first, so you know what you need help on. Telling the teacher you're completely lost might feel like the truth, but it's probably not. The more time you spend trying to diagnose the issue, the less you have for recovering the missing information.
- **Ask questions.** The quickest way to an answer is a question. If you come with questions, you can hopefully zero in on answers quickly.
- **Engage with the material.** I've had students come in for extra help—usually because their parents make them—and sit there. If I ask them what they need help with, I get a response of "nothing." That's not helping either the student or me. It's a waste of everybody's time.
- **Come often.** If you didn't understand a forty-to-sixty-minute lesson, what makes you think you'll pick it up completely in one twenty-minute extra help session? You may need to seek extra help several times in the course of any given unit.
- **Don't wait until the last minute.** It's amazing how many students seek extra help the day of a test. While I appreciate the last-minute effort, the effectiveness of the extra help session drops significantly when there's more than three people present. The more students at the session, the further divided the teacher's attention becomes. You can learn from other people's questions, but you may have to wait to ask your own questions.

I'm a huge supporter of extra help, but I'm also aware of its limitations, including the simple fact that it's not exclusive.

How does teacher given extra help differ from paid tutoring?
Extra help is not paid tutoring.

The differences:
- Paid tutors can earn upwards of $100 an hour (or more depending on the subject) to work with you exclusively for the timeframe. Extra help with your teacher is free.
- Paid tutors can help build up your confidence by showing you a different way to do something. Extra help can build up your confidence by offering you a chance to practice different problems with the same methods taught in class.
- Your tutor can help you with homework problems or concepts covered in class, but he or she probably can't predict exactly what you'll encounter on a test or quiz since he or she didn't make it.
- Your tutoring session will likely be one to one, but an extra help session is not exclusive to you.
- A paid tutor may have a different approach to problems than your teacher. This is usually fine but be aware that a difference could exist.
- Paid tutoring is typically a half-hour, an hour, or an hour and a half. I suppose it could stretch on longer, but generally, people start to fade out after an intense hour and a half. Extra help is whatever time you can squeeze in with the teacher before school, after school, or during lunch.

Nonpaid tutoring:

I received unpaid tutoring from my father for calculus and college physics. There's nothing wrong with needing help from a source that is not your teacher. Not everybody is lucky enough to have a parent capable of handling higher level math and sciences. Same goes for being able to help with writing an English paper or helping you master vocabulary for a foreign languages class.

The National Honor Society students often offer themselves up as tutors because they have a set amount of community service to do. They're usually students who have done well in the subject, but they also might not have had the same teacher as you did. The methods their teacher taught them may differ from yours. They're also only older students. They're not trained educators. Some are going to be excellent communicators, and some may understand the subject but struggle with conveying the information to you.

Friends can also be unpaid tutors. You might find them more approachable. Keep in mind you are also more likely to be distracted by having a friend as a tutor.

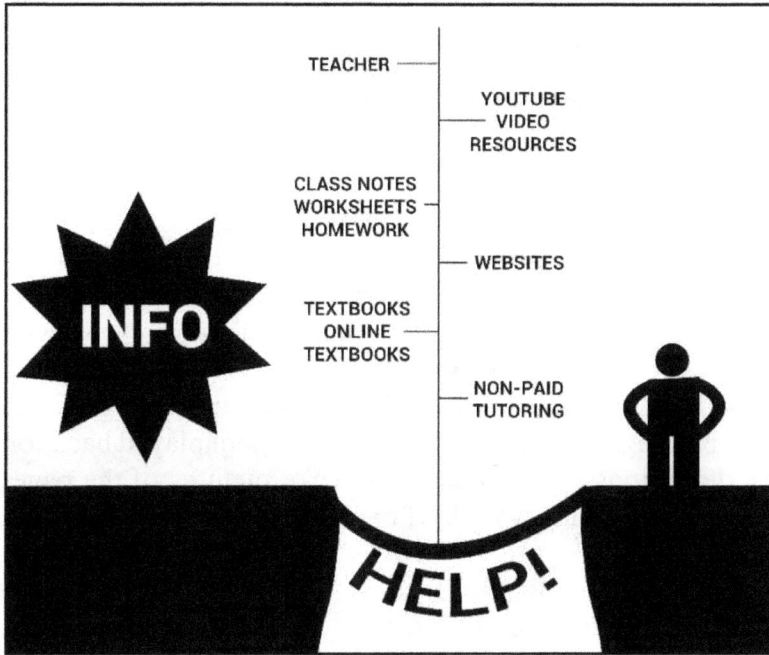

Class notes, worksheets, and homework:

The usefulness of your notes will depend heavily on your ability to take good notes. If you don't take good notes, see if a friend's notes are better and get a copy of them. You may want to interact with them by rewriting the notes, making flashcards, or typing them out.

Worksheets focus on one narrow part of the lesson. That makes them great for practicing the individual pieces but might not be the best for the big picture.

In moderation, homework offers you a chance to practice a skill on your own. As one colleague explains it, homework gives you the opportunity to test how well you know a topic. It's one thing to do problems in class with the teacher available to troubleshoot the issues when you get stuck and another for you to try it completely on your own.

Textbooks/Online Textbooks:

I cannot vouch for every textbook, but most of the ones I've worked with do an adequate job with getting the main ideas across. The push in education to get most textbooks online increases the physical accessibility but not always the mental accessibility. Like teachers, textbook authors differ in their skill level of conveying information in an understandable manner.

Reading may not be enough. Textbooks have the advantage of presenting practice question sets, often with explanations and answers. If you're truly lost, consider turning to the textbook as a resource. Consider buying an old edition of the book so you can highlight as you go. Take new notes just for the information from the textbook. If that doesn't work, find a different way to engage with the text. Try reading sections aloud and having them played back for you. Retype definitions or small sections. Take pictures of the pages and read them while taking a walk. If one method doesn't click with you, try another.

Don't be afraid to pick up a different textbook. If you don't connect with the way one author states something, check out a different book. If you get a used copy of this other textbook, you can mark it up to your heart's content.

Online textbooks make taking notes and highlighting easy. My limited exposure to online textbooks tells me they have a long way to go with making them easy to use, but they're working on that.

Websites:

Search engines are your friend, but they might not have every answer. There's a lot of information on the internet. Most of it's silly. Much of it's true and much of it is complete nonsense or blatantly false. One of the best skills you can develop as a young student is how to tell a good website from a bad one. If something ends with .edu or .gov it tends to be more reliable, but plenty of .com sites have great information too.

If you're not sure about an answer you're getting from the internet, double and triple check it with other sites. If several sites tell you the same thing, you should be fine. Pick the one that explains it the best and work with that one for your assignment.

True or false isn't the only question you should concern yourself with. You should also be aware of the target audience for each site. One meant for the general public will keep the language and presentation accessible to a middle school level. One aimed at college or Ph D students may not be as easy to comprehend.

Beware of sites that let anyone and everyone offer up an answer. Yahoo answers might be great for a quick question with a definite answer, but if you want an explanation, check a few sites. Wikipedia might be a great starting point in your information quest, but you should probably dig deeper into its sources and quote those if you're doing formal research. Same thing with a blog. Check out the credentials of the person writing the blog before using them for serious research.

YouTube and other video resources:

Most science processes have at least one YouTube video made for them. Publishers like McGraw Hill have also put up their animations as videos. These make excellent resources. The quality of YouTube videos is only as good as the content creator. Therefore, there will be everything from excellent to painful-to-watch videos.

For Chemistry, I recommend most of the Crash Course videos. I can't recommend them for any other subject as I've not watched enough of any other topic to render a judgment one way or another. For Biology, I have seen some of the Amoeba Sisters videos and they seem okay. If you have a set subject in mind, there's probably a person or company who would love to share their videos with you. Veritasium also seems to have quite a few neat science videos, but I have not seen enough of them to draw a conclusion. His videos do seem to take a unique approach to many questions. Who knows, that might be exactly what you need to grasp the topic.

Educational companies and technological advancements are making it easier for teachers to make their own videos too, so your teacher might have created some supplemental content. These would have the advantage of coming with the same language you're used to.

Even if your teacher has not created any videos, he or she may be your best resource for finding a reliable video. In preparation for their lesson, they may have already looked up some videos. If not, see if your teacher might be willing to look at a video for you and let you know if it can be trusted.

If a video's painful to watch, move on. There are plenty more out there. Several Chemistry content creators have excellent information, but I don't like their voice or the way they explain things. Those are personal issues not actual problems with the video. What bothers me may have zero impact on you, so try them anyway.

Other ways to evaluate a video resource: See how many times the video has been viewed and when it was published. If a few thousand people have watched it, you're probably okay to trust it. Check some of the comments to be sure. If two people have watched the video and one of the viewers is clearly related to the content creator, maybe move on. Then again, if the video's only a few days old, it may not have had any time to get traction, so give it a chance. Trial and error works too. If you write something you learned from a video on a test and get it wrong, ask your teacher to clarify. If the information's false, remember that before you trust another video by the same creator.

Conclusion:

Although I broke down your resources by category, likely you will need to use a combination of them to succeed. Each class might require its own mixture of teacher resources, outside resources, textbook information, website information, and video supplements.

Chapter 11:
How to Write Excellent Emails

Introduction:

I know emails are falling out of style, but they're still a useful tool for arranging meetings, asking for clarification, and making requests. Although you should avoid having the email sound like a form letter, there should be some structure to the email.

A Few Reasons to Email a Teacher:

- **Set up a meeting:** Talking over a grade and getting extra help both require you to meet the teacher. This isn't a very formal meeting, but in order for any meeting to take place, you need to find a time you're both available. Randomly popping in the teacher's room may work, but it's always nice to give the teacher advanced notice so he or she can be prepared for the encounter. This isn't as scary as it sounds. If you want to talk about a test answer, it's time efficient if the teacher already has the test out and ready for you when you get there.

- **Notification of an absence:** Whether you're going on vacation or a class trip or there's been a death in the family, you should let your teachers know when you know you're going to miss class. It shows you're responsible and gives them a chance to give you some of the makeup work. Even if you don't have time to do the work while you're away, you'll at least have it when you do get time to tackle it.

- **Asking for an extension:** This could be connected to a notification of an absence, but there are plenty of other reasons to ask for an extension on a project. Life gets complicated. Teachers try to be understanding, but powers of prediction have limitations. You don't need to go into detail concerning the *what's wrong*, but if you're asking for an extension you owe the teacher at least a brief explanation.

- **Scheduling makeups:** If you've already missed a test, you should schedule a time to make it up as soon as possible. Some students think that if they delay long enough the test just goes away. That very rarely happens. In those extreme cases where you're granted a test exemption, it's usually because things have gotten to an extremely desperate point. Usually you have to make up the test, and the more time you let pass, the worse you're going to do on the test because you'll have to balance it with the new material.

- **Asking questions about an assignment:** If you don't understand the homework, you may wish to reach out by email. Sometimes, the teacher might be able to send you a video or answer your question directly. Other times, he or she will suggest meeting in person for extra help the next day. Even if you can't finish the assignment without a more thorough answer, asking an intelligent question or two about the assignment lets the teacher know you tried to work the problem.

- **Asking for a test, project, or paper grade:** This kind of request is usually short and sweet. Be sure to give the teacher adequate time to grade the test, but if the teacher promised to have grades ready by a certain time, it's perfectly acceptable to inquire about how you did after that deadline. Many schools have online systems now, so check there first, but there's often a gap between when grades are ready and posted.

- **Grade corrections:** These should probably happen in person, but if it requires explanation first, an email is a nice starting point. Mistakes happen, and I'm happy to fix them. My records should back this up. If they do not, you'll have to be prepared to defend the grade with the actual paper or at least a picture of the paper with the grade on it. This is a good argument for don't throw stuff out until you're certain the grades are recorded correctly.

- **Grade change requests:** This is another category of questions that should be handled in person. Setting up a meeting for this over email is fine. Just be aware that working hard is what's expected of you, not a reason for magically boosting an 89 to a 90.

Overview of how to Email Adults (Specifically Teachers):
Key Points:
- Be brief.
- Be clear.
- Be polite.
- Be you.

As you get older, you should be advocating for yourself. Part of that is learning how to present yourself clearly and respectfully. Be authentic and get to your point quickly. The more you ramble, the harder it is to pick out what you're asking.

Remember, the reason you're contacting the teacher likely has something to do with you wanting something. If you want to send a random greeting email, go for it. I'm sure the teacher would love to get that little extra insight into your personality. If you're in my classes, you likely don't have a choice about that because it'll be one of your first assignments. But there's no rule about going above and beyond. Keep your email tone formal or light. You're going for clear, genuine, and polite.

Side note: Check your grammar as best you can. This is part of making a positive first impression.

Anatomy of an Effective Email:

Write a Descriptive Subject: You want your subject to be more than "yo." It doesn't have to be fancy. Something like "missing homework" or "missing class today" works perfectly fine. The more information you can fit briefly, the better, but don't worry if your subject is a tad generic.

Opening/Greeting: Start with a simple formal or casual salutation ("Dear" or "Hi"). Follow this with an appropriate title, like how you would address them in class. (Mr., Miss, Ms., or Mrs.) Spell the person's last name correctly. If you're not sure if your female teacher is married, use Ms.; it's the safest because it can apply to either.

Introduction and Background: If you're not very familiar with the teacher, introduce yourself. If you are familiar with the teacher, put a sentence or two to ease into the topic. There's a balance to strike between the need for brevity and providing enough information so the teacher fully comprehends your request. "I was out sick today" is enough. If you want to go into gory details, do so only if you have the right relationship with the teacher.

Body/Main Request: This is your main event. What do you really want or wish to know? If any section needs to be crystal clear, it's this one. Many people tend to get lost in describing the situation and not actually get to their point. Be aware of what you're asking with the request. Certain requests are more inconvenient than others. If you need to make up a test after school, that means the teacher must stay with you while you take that test.

Conclusion: This part's the winddown. Usually, a quick "Thanks for your time/ consideration/ help" works great.

Letter Closer: Sign it! Many schools provide students with school email addresses, but these might just be your first initial, last name, and graduation year. Depending on when during the school year you're sending your email, the teacher may not know who you are yet. Don't assume or get offended, just let them know your first and last name. It can help to include the period number.

Recap:
Emails should be …

☑ **Be brief.**

☑ **Be clear.**

☑ **Be polite.**

☑ **Be you.**

Conclusion:

The basic structure of the email presented will serve in multiple capacities. If you're addressing a friend, you may skip certain sections, but the structure above should work for most formal situations. When in doubt, err on the side of more formal rather than less formal. The bulk of the content in the middle is what needs to be conveyed in a face-to-face meeting as well. It never hurts to start conversations with a greeting and end with a short note of thanks. These little details may help you stand out above the rest.

Chapter 12:
Wisdom from the Collective

Introduction:

As a curious soul, I decided to ask other teachers, students, and parents their thoughts about school and communications. Everything that follows is a direct quote. My only alterations were grammatical or explanatory.

Wisdom from Current Students:

What would you like teachers to know?

"Not every student learns the same way. Some don't fit 'in the box.'" – A high school student

What would you like your fellow students to know?

"That high GPA is worth it, but don't sacrifice your life for it. Your mental health is just as important as the acceptance letters to college. That GPA covered 2 years at a community college and saved me thousands." – Dest Rose

Wisdom from Former Students:
What do you wish school taught you?
"I wish we'd studied those old dead Greek philosopher guys. I feel like that might be important stuff, but I never learned it, so I can't be sure." – Audrey Andrews

What would you like to tell students?
"Social status in high school doesn't define you for life. I had my 20th reunion last year and while I was nothing special as a teenager, I was way more awesome and confident at my reunion." – Ken Dalenberg

What advice do you have for students?
"Speak out if you get bullied, I didn't, and it ruined my life. I now have PTSD. I don't watch any bullying on TV, nor do I agree with it; it makes me so angry. So, don't be scared to speak up, get help." – Jada Sutton
Side note: Jada wants you all to know that even if you're going through some really tough things, you can make it through them, and they can ultimately make you a better person.

"Be kind to everyone, including your teachers. Be inclusive. Lift others up. By noticing someone is being left out and including them, you can make a huge difference in the life of another. Be yourself, because that is something you have that no one else will ever have and your voice is important." – Rebekah Giordano

On life beyond high school ...
"There's more to life than high school. Good things come to those who wait. The harder you work the sweeter the reward. Don't rush, savor each season of life, but be responsible." – Nicole Stuhl

On perseverance ...
"It gets better. Keep pushing through." – Danah

On peer pressure ...

"I started to smoke when I was in high school just so I could be accepted into a certain crowd. Fortunately, I quit 10 years later. It (the smoking) was a stupid move. Why do young people have to do dumb things like that to get accepted? Be yourself. Today, I don't care if people like me or not, and because I now have that attitude, I have more friends than ever before. Trying too hard to be liked never works." – Barb Goss, author

On change ...

"It's okay if you do something completely different than what you thought you would do when graduating high school. You still are a successful person even with plans changed from what they were years ago." – Laura A. Grace, author

What advice do you have for teachers and students?

"Teachers, seek to understand your students and learn how to walk miles in their shoes. Students, seek to understand your teachers and learn how to walk miles in their shoes. Understanding each other is a two-way street, so if a student is expected to understand the teacher, the teacher should also be expected to understand the student. Understanding each other is how we even begin to solve problems together. Assumptions are the enemy of understanding someone and their situation, so never assume; always ask and listen." – Christina Guglielmon

Side Note: She had a lot more to say on the subject. If you're curious, I can probably send you the entire message wherein she unpacks the statement.

Wisdom from Parents:

What would you like teachers or other parents to know?

"I'm a natural communicator, so I had no trouble approaching teachers on my own when I needed help or noticed a discrepancy that needed clarified. As a parent, I have taken my hands further off my daughter's interactions with her teachers each year, encouraging her to email them or schedule meetings with them in person. Of course, I am keeping an eye on it all, but it's crucial she learn how to advocate for herself now." – Kayla Thomas (parent of a rising 8th grader)

What would you like your children to know?

"Don't be afraid to jump from one friend group to another, or from a friend group to nothing." – Jane Lebak

What would you like other parents to know about the importance of good communication?

"Parents of high schoolers are somewhat in limbo regarding communication. We're not supposed to communicate with teachers or staff; the kids should be handling that on their own, so we're told. We just have to hope that our kids are advocating for themselves and asking the right questions. And, we certainly don't get much information from our high schoolers themselves. Therefore, if a high school teacher proactively offers communication with parents giving them updates, due dates, assignment info, etc., consider yourself lucky. Show that teacher some appreciation for that thoughtful gesture." – Debbie

Wisdom from Teachers:
You are more than a name ...
"Many of us teachers truly care about our students and will do anything in our ability to help them. All they need to do is find that one educator to whom they can confide." – Carmen Baca, former teacher of 36 years, author

Feed your brain the good stuff ...
"It's just as important to feed your brain as to feed your body. And it's just as easy to settle for junk food because it tastes good and is easy to get, but you'll be sorry later." – Kim K. O'Hara, teacher, author

Do the homework properly ... (Yes, there's a right and wrong way to do it.)
"In order to facilitate learning, I provide my students with a list of suggested homework (HW from here on out) exercises along with the solutions guide for the chapter. In discussions with students after they have not done well on an assessment, I find the following groupings: 1. HW not even attempted. 2. HW skimmed—looked at solutions guide, seems easy. 3. Relied on solutions guide in order to get through it—did not develop independence. 4. Did HW, but never consulted solutions guide for correctness—in actuality had a misconception.

Students need to realize that completing HW provides a valuable learning opportunity along with the opportunity for self-assessment. It is to their advantage to do the homework! It should be done in a timely manner so that they build up the skills and understandings needed to continually progress to the next level of learning. If students find that they must peek at the solutions guide in order to complete problems, then their learning is not yet sufficient. They should then look to complete additional problems. If they have an available textbook, often problems grouped together are similar. As a teacher, I would always be delighted to look at a student's work if the solution for a particular problem is not available. If struggling, come for extra help!" – Candy, AP Chemistry teacher

Classroom communication is important (so is understanding that home life can differ widely for your peers) ...
"After expectations and routines were established, I relaxed a bit. The door was always open. Tutoring was usually available and sometimes advice. The student body was mixed. There were a number of kids from U.N. families, and low-to upper income families, some who suffered trauma daily, others who thought trauma was marring their nail polish. I believed in communication. Opinions were not wrong and treated as a conversation opener." – C.V.

Beyond the classroom ...
"Read just for the sake of reading, not because it's assigned!" – Michael Rauseo, English teacher

Conclusion:
I realize some of these statements might seem like opposites of each other. Thank you for taking the time to take in all these different perspectives. Communication will be important throughout your life. Best of luck with your school year.

Thank You for Reading:

I hope you found something useful. If you have questions or randomly need a sympathetic stranger to talk to, feel free to reach out via email. (juliecgilbert5steps@gmail.com)

Check out some of my other works. Much of it is clean fiction, though there's also a chemistry book where I took most of the core concepts and broke them down into normal people terms. Whether you're looking for science fiction, fantasy, or mystery, I've probably got something for you. Visit my website (www.juliecgilbert.com) for audiobook samples, book descriptions, playlist links, and a peek at the pretty covers.

If you have a chemistry question, the above email also works for that. As a teacher, my one goal is to help you get the most out of your high school career.

Sincerely,

Julie C. Gilbert

Notes:

www.ingramcontent.com/pod-product-compliance
Lightning Source LLC
Chambersburg PA
CBHW071820020426
42331CB00007B/1568